Bonhoeffer and Britain

Bonhoeffer and Britain

Keith Clements

CHURCHES TOGETHER
IN BRITAIN AND IRELAND

Published in 2006 by Churches Together in Britain and Ireland
2 Paris Garden, Bastille Court, London SE1 8ND
www.ctbi/publications.org.uk
Email: info@ctbi.org.uk

ISBN 0 85169 307 5

Design and pre-press production by Heather Macpherson
and Makar Publishing Production, Edinburgh.
Jacket design by Nial Smith Design, Edinburgh.
Printed and bound in Poland. Produced by Polskabook.

Contents

Foreword

This book is a fascinating extension of what we already know about my uncle, Dietrich Bonhoeffer, through his biographies. For me especially, reading it is quite a bonus as my husband Eberhard Bethge and I lived in the same parsonage in London 20 years later, while Eberhard was doing the same kind of work as Dietrich, different though that was compared to the Nazi-time when Dietrich was there as the minister to the expatriate German congregation.

Dietrich liked London and England. When, as children, we had started to learn English in school he sometimes addressed us in English and was pleased when we understood what he had said or could even answer him in English.

When Eberhard and I came to London there were still people (featured in this book) who had been so important to Dietrich especially during the Church Struggle, like Bishop Bell of Chichester, or Joe Oldham. Oldham was very interested in European affairs and especially German affairs. He had helped already in the First World War to prevent the British Government from confiscating the property of the German missions in British territories and he kept himself informed about foreign matters. He was especially interested in the Church Struggle.

While in London, Dietrich was kept informed about the Church Struggle by his parents (mainly his mother) and some friends in Berlin. In order to get the most recent news he had to phone Berlin often. His friend Franz Hildebrandt, who for a while lived with Dietrich in London, told us the nice story that one day the telephone bill was so high that Dietrich could not pay it. So the two friends decided to go to the phone office. There was a nice lady who saw that the bill could not be paid and she halved it for them!

So, while in London Dietrich always had news about what was happening in Germany in the church and in politics. When he was back in Germany he was sent to England several times in order to share breaking news. As Keith Clements writes, "for a few weeks Bonhoeffer must have wondered whether he had really left his London pastorate."

Dietrich had brought many of his ideas on how to run his seminary for students of the "illegal" Confessing Church from England. He was called back to Germany to do this. He had visited some Anglican seminaries and monasteries, for instance Mirfield, which had impressed him, as in such places theological preparation was done in relation to the churches and not mainly by the university as it was in Germany. And Dietrich believed that this was a reason for the breakdown of the church in Germany.

This is just one example of how much, as told in this book, Dietrich Bonhoeffer owed to Britain, and I hope it will find many grateful readers both in Britain and the wider world.

Renate Bethge

Preface and Acknowledgements

The year 2006 sees the centenary of the birth of Dietrich Bonhoeffer, whose repute as a seminal theologian and as a martyr for truth and justice is beyond question. This book is an illustrated account focusing on one particular feature of the Bonhoeffer story: his relationships with the people and churches of Britain. As such the book seeks to fulfil several needs.

In the first place, the engagement of Bonhoeffer with the British scene and with British people was of central significance to him throughout the last fourteen years of his life, right to the very eve of his execution at Flossenbürg concentration camp in April 1945. Yet it has not generally been highlighted as fully as it deserves. His relationship with Bishop George Bell is well-known as one of the outstanding points in the ecumenical story of the 20th century. But many other British figures were part of the Bonhoeffer drama. Much of that drama was of course fatefully played out in Germany, but some of the most vital scenes were set in England - and not only during his eighteen months as a pastor in London 1933-35.

Second, the very fact of Bonhoeffer's elevation to the status of heroic martyr or even to a kind of sainthood carries the danger that we lose sight of his real human-ity and the earthy context in which he lived and worked. Bonhoeffer's statue now rightfully stands with those of nine other 20th century Christian martyrs high above the west door of Westminster Abbey. But he actually walked below, on the streets of London and many other places in Britain. The passage of time, too, encourages for later generations an impression of detachment from the scene in which he lived. Too often portrayals of Bonhoeffer focus on the man himself as if he was a kind of lone ranger acting out his costly obedience to God in holy isolation. But he could not have done what he did without the involvement of many other figures, some of whom were not just a supporting cast but had vital roles of their own in the drama as whole. To emphasize the role of the British actors is one way of making this clear, and also brings to light a range of remarkable men and women of the 1930s and 1940s whose memory needs to be reinstated for the present generation.

Third, telling the Bonhoeffer story in this way should encourage people in Britain to appreciate more fully the value of certain features in their own cultural and religious heritage. Far from inculcating a kind of de-valuation of themselves or even a kind of inferiority complex, admiration of a figure like Bonhoeffer should lead us to ask why this great German should himself have appreciated and loved so much in the British way of life. The continuity of many traditions, the relaxed and relatively tolerant attitude to different points of view, the openness to foreigners and a real interest in the outside world (especially by the churches), and even the typical British "reserve" in human relationships, were all features with which he empathized and that he cherished. Above all, he came to owe much to the creative diversity of British church life. He drew inspiration alike from Anglicans (high and low), Baptists, Methodists, Presbyterians and Quakers. Britain provided him with a milieu vital for invigorating his work in Germany, and it would be a good question to ask whether it would do so again today or whether some of the values he so much appreciated are in danger of being eroded.

Fourth, if as is hoped this book will be read in the English-speaking world beyond the shores of Britain, it should encourage admirers of Bonhoeffer not to overlook these islands either in their survey of his story or in their attempts actually to "retrace the steps of Bonhoeffer". Many North Americans for example make pilgrimages to Europe and visit the prime Bonhoeffer sites of Berlin, Finkenwalde, Buchenwald, Flossenbürg and so forth. It is not simply with the aim of boosting the British tourist industry but in the hope of offering a fuller picture of Bonhoeffer's own pilgrimage that they are invited also to include Britain in their itineraries. London, Cambridge, Oxford, Selly Oak, Bradford, Mirfield and Edinburgh are just some of the sites on offer (and they have certain other attractions besides!).

Finally there is an unashamedly ulterior motive behind this book. It is intended to accompany the publication by Fortress Press in 2006 of the English version of Volume 13 *London 1933-35*, in the new critical edition of the entire works of Dietrich Bonhoeffer. It is hoped that reading this present book, while it deals with a span of his life much longer than his London period, will encourage readers to turn for themselves to the complete collection of all Bonhoeffer's surviving London letters, papers and sermons that is now becoming available in English for the first time. They will discover for themselves the intensity and richness of his output while a pastor in England, and how decisive that time was for his part in the Christian witness against Nazism.

Some explanation on two points of terminology in the following pages may be helpful. First, "evangelical" when used in relation to the German church scene generally means "Protestant" as distinct from Catholic, rather than "evangelical" as used in the Anglo-Saxon milieu to denote Protestants with a conservative biblical or "low church" bent. Second, it will be noticed that the name of the church that formed itself in opposition to the nazification of Christianity in Germany is variously given as the "Confessing" or "Confessional Church". It is now generally accepted that the truer English rendering of *Bekennende Kirche* is "Confessing Church". But many writers of the time used the term "Confessional", including Bonhoeffer himself when writing in English, and when such writings are cited that term is kept as originally written.

In order to avoid the appearance of an overly academic work I have avoided the use of notes for references. A full list of sources however is given in the bibliography and the enthusiastic reader should have little difficulty in finding the precise location of citations.

This book, though relatively short, could not have been produced without the assistance of many collaborators whose helpfulness I gratefully acknowledge. In particular, chapter 3 dealing with Bonhoeffer's London pastorate draws much upon the English edition of Volume 13, *London 1933-35*, in the Dietrich Bonhoeffer Works series, of which it has been my privilege to be editor. I greatly appreciate the readiness of the General Editor of the series, Victoria Barnett, and Michael West of Fortress Press, to allow citations from the text in advance of the actual publication of the volume, and of course I express gratitude to my Geneva colleague Isabel Best, the translator of the German material in that volume.

Many other individuals have put me in their debt. First of all I must thank members of my family: my wife Margaret who not only had to put up with my indulgence in yet another "Bonhoeffer enterprise" but helped to uncover some finer historical and geographical points in the story, not to mention casting a critical eye over the manuscript on behalf of the "general reader"; my son Peter and his wife Laura for extra work with the camera; and my son Jonathan who used his journalistic skills to track down vital records in London that in turn led to some new contacts relating to Bonhoeffer's pastoral work. Pride of place among these must go to Rita Colman, daughter of Frank and Doris Goetz whose wedding Bonhoeffer conducted in 1934 at the St Paul's Church, and her son Paul Colman. Rita Colman passed on some of her family's reminiscences of Bonhoeffer and of that occasion, and moreover supplied two photographs of the wedding, one of them including the pastor at the reception. Not only is this a hitherto unknown picture of Bonhoeffer to appear in public but it is, as far as I know, almost the only one of him wearing anything approximating to formal clerical dress!

Others who have kindly supplied photographs, often with accompanying information, of members of their family or community, are: Ben Buxton; Bettina Gordon; Brother Steven Haws (Community of the Resurrection, Mirfield); Christopher Hodgson; Dr Peter Hughes (Society of the Sacred Mission); George Mallinckrodt KBE (President of Schroders plc); Sir John Moberly; and George Wedell. The Dietrich Bonhoeffer Kirche at Sydenham and the German Church in Bradford (Pastor Martin Günther) have made photographs available. To all these I am grateful, as to others who have given help and advice in tracing sources and photographs: Richard Bingle; Martin Conway; Christian Gremmels; Stephen Plant; Anne Thomson (Archivist, Newnham College, Cambridge); and the Rt Revd Peter Walker. Mention too must be made of the *Methodist Recorder* and several of its readers who helped me identify John Wright on the group photograph of Richmond College (Bill Jones, John Long, Brian Newbold, John and Margaret Pearson, Ruth Picksley). Any others, whom I have overlooked but who deserve mention, please receive my apologies.

A number of institutions have not only enabled this work but have been positively helpful and encouraging: Lewisham Local Studies Centre; the Library of King's College, Cambridge; Spurgeon's College, London; the archival services of the Dioceses of Ripon and of Gloucester; the John Rylands Library University of Manchester; the Photographic Section, Imperial War Museum; the National Newspaper Library, Colindale; the Handschriftabteilung, Staatsbibliothek in Berlin; Lambeth Palace Library (in particular the Assistant Archivist Clare Brown); the National Portrait Gallery; and the Library and Archives of the World Council of Churches, Geneva. A full list of credits and permissions for the photographs is found at the end of the book.

It is one thing to obtain photographs, but quite another to prepare their reproduction for publication. A huge debt is due to Michael Bray, a friend and colleague over many years, who devoted countless hours and immense care to this side of the work in addition to taking a good number of photographs himself. He quite justifiably says that he did not realise quite what he was taking on at the beginning, but I am sure that readers will be glad he did so.

The poem "Christmas Trees" (page 126), from the *Collected Poems* of Christopher Hill is copyright Penguin (UK) Publications, and is reprinted by permission of the author and publisher.

Not all the sources drawn upon are in printed form, whether verbal or photographic. Acknowledgement is made to BBC Religious Programmes for the use of recorded reminiscences of Bonhoeffer by Mrs Henrietta Bell and Squadron Leader Hugh Falconer that have featured in a number of radio documentaries over the years. With the passage of time the people who can directly recall Dietrich Bonhoeffer are diminishing in number, but there are still surprises. For example Fred Collins, a senior member of Perry Rise Baptist Church, has come up with a quite vivid memory of Bonhoeffer preaching from that pulpit over 70 years ago. There is, above all, one special source of anecdotal recollection that I have had the privilege of absorbing almost unconsciously for some thirty years: many conversations with the late Eberhard Bethge, Dietrich Bonhoeffer's closest friend and biographer, and his wife Renate, Bonhoeffer's niece. It is therefore an added grace that Renate Bethge has kindly written the foreword.

Finally, a book requires a publisher. It was Simon Barrow, at that time responsible for publications in Churches Together in Britain and Ireland (CTBI), who first encouraged me in my idea for this project and together we laid out its basic shape. His successor Janet de Vigne has energetically taken up the baton and devoted her best efforts to seeing it into print in a very short space of time, and I am most grateful. That it is being published by the overall ecumenical body for the British Isles will, I hope, encourage a greater awareness that the ecumenical journey is one that continually needs the inspiration and example manifested in such as Dietrich Bonhoeffer.

Keith Clements
Geneva, Advent 2005

CHAPTER 1

A SCENE IN BERLIN

It is a summer day in 1931. On the front door-step of a large house in the leafy Grunewald district of Berlin stands a 25 year-old man, tall and strongly built with fairish hair, his broad face wearing an intent but friendly expression. He is accompanied by several heavy cases. Dietrich Bonhoeffer has returned to his family home in the Wangenheimstrasse after a year away in New York. Karl and Paula Bonhoeffer warmly greet their youngest son, doubtless wondering, as all parents would, if he's changed at all.

Naturally they would not have cause to know that his English has improved almost to perfection (though inevitably, as so often with German academics, spoken with a slight American accent). But they would know from his letters home that America had intrigued and excited him far more than he had expected when he set sail westwards a year ago, and he would have much to tell them. They would be preparing themselves for some surprises as to what he felt were the most significant experiences and discoveries. But then, Dietrich always has surprised them right from the time when as a young boy he announced that he wanted to be a theologian and pastor. Their other sons had chosen very different careers – his older brothers Karl-Friedrich and Klaus had opted for physics and law respectively. The other brother, Walter, lay in a war-grave. The nearest any of his siblings came to a similar choice to Dietrich's was when his younger sister Susanne married a theologian, Walter Dress. His twin-sister Sabine and the older sisters Ursula and Christine all married lawyers.

In fact the boy Dietrich at one stage seemed destined to be a concert pianist, such was the musical talent he showed. But his parents had not protested at his own choice. Karl Bonhoeffer, the eminent professor of psychiatry at the Charité Clinic in Berlin, was agnostic in matters of religion but deeply respectful of people's sincere convictions and was always to be quietly supportive of his son's aspirations. Paula Bonhoeffer, who came from an aristocratic background, was devout and saw to a typically Lutheran brand of family piety in the home. She was already taking an intense interest in Dietrich's theological journey.

Dietrich Bonhoeffer, 1930-31

And what an extraordinary journey that has already proved to be! Dietrich began his studies at the age of seventeen in Tübingen, and then continued in Berlin. At the mere age of 21 he gained his doctorate. That was remarkable in itself, but the thesis he had written and published as *Sanctorum Communio* was many years later to be called by the greatest theologian of the 20th century, Karl Barth, "a theological miracle". Unpacking that statement, like Dietrich's traveling cases, can wait a minute or two. Three years later, in 1930, he had qualified as a university lecturer with his "habilitation" thesis, *Akt und Sein (Act and Being),* an equally rigorous argument with the leading theological and philosophical trends of the day. As if all this is not enough, for a young German of his time he has an unusually wide experience of the world outside the Fatherland. Between Tübingen and Berlin he spent several months in Rome, falling in love with the classical sites and moved almost to distraction by the Easter liturgy in St Peter's, where for the first time he glimpsed what the truly universal community of the church might look like, gathered from the four corners of the earth. Not only so, but from there with his brother Klaus he took off south to Sicily and beyond . . . to the sands, kasbahs and mosques of Libya. Then, in 1928, after some time as assistant to one of the professors in Berlin, he went for a year to Spain, as assistant pastor to the German congregation in Barcelona. Among the surprises he produced for his family there was his evident enjoyment of the bullfight, which he defended as an antidote to a prevailing "gloomy" brand of Catholicism.

At 25, unknown to himself or anyone else, Dietrich Bonhoeffer has only another fourteen years to live. But he has already a breadth of experience unknown to many people twice his age, aided by a capacity to enter into and empathize with social scenes and cultures very different from home. So now, doubtless over coffee and cakes on the Grunewald lawn, he starts to regale his family with his American experiences: the hedonism of Broadway contrasting with the desperate poverty so manifest on the lesser sidewalks, occasioned by the Wall Street crash of 1929; the illogicality of capitalistic free enterprise coinciding with the "prohibition" laws against alcohol; the liberal atmosphere and informality of teaching methods at Union Theological

Seminary, so different from the strict precision of the German faculties, and much else . . . But perhaps nothing is more surprising than when he begins to talk about his discovery of black America, its suffering, its struggles and its spirituality. His gateway into this world was the Abyssinian Baptist Church in Harlem. He had been taken one Sunday by a black student at Union, Frank Fisher. There, Dietrich says, for the first time in New York, bestrewn with comfortable middle-class white churches, he had really heard the gospel of Christ preached at full power and the praises of God sung with real fervour. It became his spiritual home in New York and he taught a Sunday school class for several weeks. He unpacks from one of his cases some gramophone records. At Wangenheimstrasse the standard musical fare is Bach chorales and Beethoven sonatas, but soon the drawing room is filled with *Swing low, sweet chariot* and other spirituals.

So, his parents conclude, Dietrich is still much the same: intellectually rigorous as ever yet excited by new experiences and prepared to defend the unexpected. But there is something more, a hint of a new kind of seriousness that they cannot quite identify, a suspicion of a new sort of question troubling him that he is not yet ready to declare openly because he himself is not sure how to answer it. That too can wait a moment.

Meanwhile, he in turn wants to know from the parents if and how Germany has changed during this year. They look concerned. The news is not all good. The Weimar Republic, Germany's first real experiment in democracy, is in deepening trouble economically, socially and politically. The National Socialist Party of Adolf Hitler is gaining ground. Even in the universities the signs are ominous, not least in the theological faculties. Nazi gangs have been attacking Jewish students and professors suspected of being left-wing or unpatriotic are publicly abused, with demands for their dismissal.

This is not an outwardly promising context for a return to academic life. Dietrich Bonhoeffer is clearly a rising star on the theological horizon in Berlin. An assured post as lecturer in systematic theology awaits him, to be followed no doubt in due course by a professorship. The church, too, is very interested in him. He has always wanted to be a pastor as well as an academic and he is due for ordination in the autumn. Why such high expectations of him in so many areas? Here we must look back to his two published theses, *Sanctorum Communio* and *Akt und Sein*. They are not the easiest reading, but at their core lie crucial issues to which Bonhoeffer has given not only his mind but his heart – and that, arguably, will lead ultimately to his death.

Protestant theology from the mid-nineteenth century had increasingly concentrated on the phenomena of the religious life, one might say the *human* aspects of faith: the church in its many forms as a historical institution; faith as an *experience* of spiritual uplift and moral endeavour; the "kingdom of God" as the gradual progress of enlightened "civilization" and culture. Christianity was equated with "culture-Protestantism", an amalgam of western scientific and moral idealism flavoured with biblical-sounding notes about the brotherhood of mankind and the communion of the soul with the fatherly God. This was "liberal Protestantism." Then came the disaster of 1914-18 when this "Christian civilization" in Europe collapsed in blood and slaughter. It was a young Swiss Reformed pastor, Karl Barth, who sounded the call to a reverse direction in theology in his commentary *The Epistle to the Romans* and his subsequent works as a professor in Germany in the 1920s. Barth was appalled by the way so many liberal theologians actually *hailed* the

"Kaiser's war" as a fight for Christianity. This showed that Protestantism had lost its soul. It had been talking about human religiosity, human ethical idealism, human culture when it should have been talking about *God*, and the *word of God* which is not another term for human religiosity but is *wholly other* to everything human including – and especially – "religion". Theology had to be re-founded on the biblical message that runs counter to every human insight and aspiration: the "impossible possibility" that a new creation comes solely through Christ, crucified and resurrected and the power of the age to come, the Holy Spirit.

Karl Barth

Germany in the 1920s became a battleground between this new "theology of crisis" or "dialectical theology" and the older liberal theology. The young Dietrich Bonhoeffer soon became a passionate convert to the Barthian way. But he was not so fanatical as to ignore the valid insights of the older liberal school, still very prevalent in Berlin. Adolf von Harnack, one of the greatest church historians of all time, remained his revered teacher. Essentially, what Dietrich Bonhoeffer sought to do in *Sanctorum Communio* and *Akt und Sein* was to affirm what Barth was saying about the "wholly otherness" of God while at the same time recognizing that God *is* known in very concrete human experience. In effect Barth was saying "God can *only* be known in Jesus Christ." Bonhoeffer was wanting to say, "I agree. But *how* is this Jesus Christ known? *Where* do we actually meet him?" His own answer was: in the community of the church. "The church is Christ existing as community." Here, revelation becomes concrete. We encounter God in sociality, in an experience of community where the forgiveness of sins is practised.

This young theologian was somewhat of a puzzle to his seniors: too Barthian for the liberals, too sociologically concerned for the Barthians. But they felt he had important, unifying things to say in what threatened to become an increasingly polarized context. He was a wanted man, both in the church and in the university. His plans were becoming clearer: to begin work as an assistant pastor or student chaplain, and to start lecturing in the faculty of theology.

But first he has other things to do. He will soon be visiting Karl Barth, now professor in Bonn, for the first time. With his friend Franz Hildebrandt he will start to write a new Lutheran catechism. And something else comes up. Superintendent Max Diestel (in overall charge of Bonhoeffer's preparation for ordination) is, in addi-

tion to his responsibilities in the Berlin church, much involved with international ecumenical activities, and from his office much of the German work of the World Alliance for Promoting International Friendship through the Churches is carried out. The World Alliance will be holding a major conference in Cambridge, England, early in September. Would Dietrich Bonhoeffer be willing to go as one of the German youth delegates? The answer comes quickly: yes.

Franz Hildebrandt

Here too is something of a surprise for those who thought they knew Dietrich Bonhoeffer. As a staunchly academic Lutheran, he had hitherto – so they assumed – exhibited a typical caution towards well-meaning but theologically dubious attempts at "building the kingdom of God" on earth. Anglo-Saxon, liberal Protestantism seemed to set more store by human idealism rather than a proper, reverential expectancy for action from God's side. The Sermon on the Mount, in the typical Lutheran understanding, was not intended as a practical guide to living in a sinfully imperfect world, but was Christ's way of telling us how impossible it was to live a righteous life by our own efforts and therefore we simply had to beg for God's mercy and forgiveness. But in America Bonhoeffer had had his eyes opened, not just by the teaching of Reinhold Niebuhr on Christian social ethics, not just by the social activism of the American churches and not even solely by his encounter with the black experience. For the first time in his life he had met and made friends with a thorough-going pacifist, and moreover a Frenchman, representative of a country with which Germany had been so bitterly at war. Jean Lasserre, a young Reformed pastor also studying at Union Seminary, had begun to stir up a new question in Bonhoeffer's mind: maybe Jesus did, after all, mean exactly what he said in calling for love for our enemies, for turning the other cheek, for answering hatred and violence with forgiveness. In *Sanctorum Communio* and *Akt und Sein* the young Lutheran had argued for revelation as earthed in concrete action and community. There is where Jesus Christ is met. But what could be more concrete than obeying the exact commands of Jesus, actually to *follow* him and not just lecture about him, in a violent world?

This is what lies behind that new, brooding, disturbed seriousness with which Dietrich Bonhoeffer sips his coffee on his parents' lawn. He is about to embark on yet another journey, to absorb another world of experience. And a lot of that way will now lie through Britain.

CHAPTER 2

CAMBRIDGE 1931

For a certain category of people, of course, there could be no better place than Cambridge for an introduction to the English scene. The week he spent here in September 1931 would certainly have given Dietrich Bonhoeffer much to muse over enjoyably as each morning he walked from Ridley Hall along the tree-lined Backs, past the soaring splendour of King's Chapel and then over the Cam and into Trinity Great Court. But Cambridge is not just alluring scenery. It is itself a stage; the setting for an endless chain of human dramas over the centuries: intellectual discoveries, personal encounters and life-changing decisions. To these dramas must be added that of Dietrich Bonhoeffer, for it was in Cambridge that he consciously entered international ecumenical activity with a specific and continuing responsibility. It was this involvement that within a few years was to prove vital for his leading role in the German Church Struggle. More fatefully still, from 1940 it was this engagement and the foreign contacts it had given him that he was to put at the service of the resistance to Hitler. Cambridge is therefore a point on the pilgrimage that leads to the execution yard at Flossenbürg.

The World Alliance for Promoting International Friendship through the Churches had grown out of exchange visits between German and British church representatives during 1908-09, starting a burgeoning movement soon joined by French, Scandinavian and North American delegates. It had held its official inaugural meeting at Constance on 1 August 1914 – with a tragic irony just as Europe was mobilizing for war. After the four years of bloodletting, the World Alliance, tentatively at first, resumed its meetings. The delicate process of rapprochement between the former belligerents – especially Germany, France and Britain – and the treatment of religious minorities within the new national borders of Europe were its first priorities. It grew in strength and in the breadth of its membership which, while overwhelmingly European and North American, was joined by China, India and Japan. Other ecumenical actors of course were on the scene: the International Missionary Council (formed in 1921) carrying on the work begun by the World Missionary Conference of Edinburgh in

The Cambridge Backs: King's and Clare Colleges

1910; the Universal Christian Council for Life and Work, formed at the Stockholm Conference of 1927; and the Faith and Order movement (Lausanne, 1927). Compared with these, the World Alliance was a less official body. Membership of it was a matter of personal interest and commitment rather than official representation of the churches – though those members were often prominent people on their home scene (German academics and British and American bishops, in particular). Its dominant ethos was liberal, western Protestantism rather than teutonic intellectuality; moral pragmatism rather than theological analysis of the human condition. *How* to stop another war was its main question, and its answer was already given in its name: by promoting friendly relations between nations through meetings and conferences, first among the churches, and then through the churches exercising moral persuasion on their peoples and governments. Cambridge 1931 was to be its eighth conference and by now the main focus was on the need for disarmament, with high hopes and anxieties awaiting the World Disarmament Conference set to begin in Geneva in February 1932.

In the light of all this it was, again, something of a surprise that Dietrich Bonhoeffer should have readily accepted to attend the Cambridge conference at Superintendent Diestel's invitation. There seemed precious little theological basis to the work of the World Alliance, and the passing of high-sounding resolutions at international meetings too often seemed like moralizing self-indulgence and the evasion of truly concrete action. But, quite apart from his stirring interest in peace questions, two things seemed to have appealed to Bonhoeffer in this invitation: first, his appetite already whetted by America and his earlier travels, there was the chance it offered for still further international encounters and contacts; second, the lack of any true theology in the World Alliance might have constituted a kind of missionary call to him, to help supply one.

So, sometime in the second half of August 1931 Bonhoeffer set off for England. It is not exactly true to say that Cambridge was his very first encounter with Britain – or at least the British. At Union Seminary in New York two of his teachers were Scottish: the New Testament scholar James Moffat and the professor of systematic theology John Baillie. With Baillie there began a lasting friendship. Baillie, till then a personalist theologian in liberal vein, was intrigued by this passionate disciple and advocate of Karl Barth. It was through Bonhoeffer that Baillie had one of his first encounters with the continental "theology of crisis". After his return to Edinburgh in 1934 Baillie was to become one of the most creative theologians on the British scene, and would be powerfully involved in the ecumenical movement. His book *Our Knowledge of God* (1939) contains what is probably the first reference to

John Baillie

and citation from Bonhoeffer's *Akt und Sein* in a British publication. At Union Seminary Bonhoeffer also met Reinhold Niebuhr's English wife Ursula (although, reportedly, she did not take too warmly to what appeared to her an embodiment of upper-class German formality and intellectual superiority). But in Niebuhr's classes he had also met a certain amount of modern English literature, including some of the plays of George Bernard Shaw (whom he found too cynical) and R.C. Sheriff's *Journey's End* which impressed him greatly by its depiction alike of idealism and the harsh reality of trench warfare. The memory of his brother Walter, killed in 1918 on the western front, must have been a factor here.

Nor is it quite the case that Cambridge was his first taste of England. Just prior to the conference itself there were preliminary youth and student meetings at two seaside resorts, St-Leonard's-on-Sea on the south coast in Sussex, and at Westcliffe-on-Sea in Essex. Very little is known of what happened at these meetings, but they provided Bonhoeffer with his first meeting with one of the major English figures in the World Alliance, Edward Arthur Burroughs, Bishop of Ripon from 1926 until his death in 1934. Burroughs was president of the British council of the World Alliance and therefore heavily involved in the planning of the Cambridge conference.

Edward Arthur Burroughs, Bishop of Ripon

Ridley Hall

Some 300 delegates from 30 countries assembled in Cambridge for the opening of the conference on 1 September. Trinity, the largest of the colleges, accommodated the male adults, while the Presbyterian (now United Reformed) Westminster College hosted the women. The youth delegates, Bonhoeffer among them, were quartered at the customary safe distance away in Ridley Hall, the low-church Anglican theological college off Sidgwick Avenue, and had a preparatory conference of their own for two days prior to the opening of the main event. At 3.00 p.m. on Tuesday 1 September the gathering convened in the Examination Schools in Benet Street (where all the plenary sessions would be held) for the official opening under the chairmanship of Arthur Burroughs, flanked by dignitaries of town and gown. A loyal address was telegraphed to King George V. Lord Willoughby Hyett Dickinson (chairman of London County Council and president of the World Alliance) read out messages from the Archbishop of Canterbury, other national church leaders and Arthur Henderson, chairman of the disarmament conference. The master of Downing College conveyed the welcome from the university. The rural dean of Cambridge, S.T. Adams, and the minister of St Andrews Street Baptist Church, Robert Child, spoke for the Church of England and free churches respectively. After dinner came the opening service in the chapel of Trinity College. Miles Krumbine

Trinity Great Court

of Cleveland, Ohio, preached the sermon. "The will to war," he declared, "will break down when war no longer serves national interests. That hour has come at last . . . It is just as logical and timely for the statesman of today to plot peace in the interest of his nation as it seemed necessary to the statesman of the nineteenth century to plot war."

It was precisely this kind of optimistic pragmatism that drew Bonhoeffer's criticism of the non-theological ethos of the World Alliance. With another youth delegate, Pierre Toureille of France, he was scornful of the poster that welcomed delegates to Cambridge: "World Peace depends on World Disarmament and Disarmament depends on you!" There was plenty more in the same vein in Cambridge during the next five days: speech after speech, sermon after sermon, on disarmament as a moral issue, as a challenge to the churches, as a factor in national security and so on. And of course there were the resolutions passed at the business session on the penultimate day, the main one being on disarmament. After stating ". . . [W]ar considered as an institution for the settlement of international disputes is incompatible with the mind and method of Christ therefore is incompatible with the mind and method of His Church" the declaration went on to welcome the summoning of the world disarmament conference; to demand a substantial reduction of armaments in every form, the fixing of a scale for the armed forces of the nations, and security for all nations against aggression . . . it was passed unanimously. Disarmament had become a highly sore issue for the German delegates even before the conference began. During the weeks leading up to Cambridge two prominent German theologians, Paul Althaus and Emmanuel Hirsch, had launched a vicious attack on the World Alliance and on all such international ecumenical gatherings, accusing any Germans who participated in them of virtual treason against the Fatherland: ". . . a Christian and church understanding and cooperation on the questions of rapprochement among the peoples is impossible as long as the others are waging a murderous policy against our people." In the climate encouraged by this attack, to be a German present at all in Cambridge required significant courage. In fact the German delegates felt they could not speak publicly on the disarmament issue – though they all, Bonhoeffer included, supported the World Alliance resolution.

World Alliance garden party, Christ's College. Bonhoeffer can be seen at the extreme left on the back row, looking away to his left

The days in Cambridge were not of course occupied solely by speeches and debate. There was a service of prayer each morning in Trinity Chapel. There was time for sightseeing, to admire the Wren Library at Trinity, to gaze at the glass in King's Chapel, to look around the Fitzwilliam Museum. On the Thursday afternoon there was a garden party in the grounds of Christ's College hosted by "United Christian Witness in Cambridge". And as always, there was time for unplanned but often useful personal and informal conversations. For Bonhoeffer it was the encounter with his French counterparts that remained a priority. There were still many unhealed memories from 1914-18. But one wonders, too, how far he mused on matters of economics. During 1930-32 the issues of disarmament, trade and repayments of debts by the allies to the USA were all enmeshed together – with the question of German payment of war reparations at the centre of it all. Prior to Cambridge, Bonhoeffer had tried to get himself up to speed on these issues by a lot of reading. Perhaps, as he wandered around Cambridge, the name of John Maynard Keynes was mentioned to him. The Cambridge don who was to become the leading economist of the mid-century had first made his mark with the dissertation that earned him his fellowship of King's College, warning on the economic consequences of the Versailles peace.

Bonhoeffer in Cambridge therefore found himself beginning a dual role: critical of the World Alliance for its theological shallowness, yet at the same time feeling called to stand by it and defend it against the virulent, right-wing nationalist hostility it was receiving at home. That is why, towards the end of the week, he readily agreed to be appointed as one of three new honorary youth secretaries for the World Alliance. His responsibility would be for Germany, central and northern Europe, Hungary and Austria, His French friend Toureille was appointed to cover elsewhere in Europe and Latin America, while Tom Craske (English) dealt with Britain, Europe and the Far East. It was not as though Bonhoeffer would not already have enough on his plate, as university lecturer, student chaplain and pastor. That he not only took on this extra responsibility but devoted himself to it unreservedly for the next two years and more, shows what a serious commitment he was making. But it was also to bring significant rewards in terms of influential contacts. As an official of the World Alliance he would now be placed in direct touch not only with senior figures in Berlin such as Friedrich Siegmund-Schultze, editor of *Die Eiche*, the impressive and widely- read journal of the ecumenical peace movement, but with international figures outside Germany too. As a youth secretary, he would now also attend meetings of the management committee and council of the World Alliance as an *ex officio* member without embarrassing questions being asked in Germany about his being a German representative. He would be in direct contact with people such as Louis Henriod, the Geneva-based secretary both of the World Alliance and Life and Work. In fact, as the work of the World Alliance and that of the Universal Council for Life and Work became ever more closely coordinated (their respective executive committees often being held coincidentally and some of their leaders active in both organizations) it was this connection above all that was now going to prove significant in Bonhoeffer's future course. He was on the path that would bring him close to Bishop George Bell and the very centre of decision-making in the ecumenical movement. He was, moreover, encouraged by the way the World Alliance was now giving a greater place to youth. It was he and Toreille who prepared the youth delegates' message to the conference as a whole, expressing deep gratitude for the whole experience yet also – characteristically for Bonhoeffer – with the rider that: "Humanitarian efforts will never make war disappear, the struggle against it must come out of different depths and greater obedience."

The fullest significance of all this may not have been apparent when the Cambridge conference closed. At 5:30 p.m. on Friday 4 September the procession formed up in Trinity Great Court and slowly wound along Trinity Street, each delegation following a placard bearing the name of its country, and then turned into

Procession to Great St Mary's for the closing service: the Danish contingent arrives

Great St Mary's, the University Church, for the closing service. Arthur Burroughs preached the sermon, on Isaiah 2:5: "O, house of Jacob, come ye and let us walk in the light of the Lord." It was a call to total conversion for churches, governments and no less for individual Christians. The real enemy was not war, but the selfishness which issues in war. His final peroration touched a note which, now with hindsight, seems ominously prophetic – the churches' witness for peace would open the way to martyrdom. "It will be for every Christian in that way to decide between two forms of treason, treason to God or treason to the State. Are we preparing ourselves and

Great St Mary's

our peoples for that decision?" Great St Mary's that evening rang with Luther's *Ein' feste Burg ist unser Gott* sung in German. But among the other hymns printed for use during the conference was the English version of the Danish B.S. Ingemann's "Through the night of doubt and sorrow", whose penultimate verse – in its final two lines especially – might serve as the signature to the commitment Bonhoeffer was now sealing through prayer in Great St Mary's:

> *One the strain that lips of thousands*
>   *Lift as from the heart of one;*
> *One the conflict, one the peril,*
>   *One the march in God begun.*

CHAPTER 3

THE LONDON PASTOR
1933-35

The eighteen months that Dietrich Bonhoeffer spent as pastor in London from October 1933 to April 1935 are apt to be overlooked as a mere interlude in the "real" dramas that he was engaged with in Germany. For example, Martin Doblmeier's otherwise excellent documentary film *Bonhoeffer* affords this episode just a few seconds, apart from what took place at the ecumenical conference in Fanø, Denmark, in August 1934. Bonhoeffer himself in a letter to his brother Karl-Friedrich said he felt it to be an "intermezzo", but as a musician he would know that such a stage can be important in the work as a whole. In fact far from being an off-stage diversion, Bonhoeffer's London period is central to his story. His involvement in the German Church Struggle not only continued but unexpectedly intensified in London, and it was a vital time of preparation for what was to follow when he returned to Germany in 1935. If he had not spent these months in London, he would not have become such a close and trusted friend of Bishop George Bell, in a relationship that was to be crucial alike for the German church opposition, the ecumenical movement and, finally, the political resistance. If he had not been in London for this length of time, outside the oppressive constraints of Germany, he would not have had the opportunity to study the possibilities of non-violent resistance to the extent that he did. Had he not been in England for this time, he would not have learnt from its rich diversity of confessional and denominational church life and especially from the varied forms of theological education, which was to prove vital for his future work in the Confessing Church. But for this opportunity of furthering his own pastoral experience with the charge of two local congregations he could hardly have stood before his future ordinands at Finkenwalde with much credibility. Finally, working as intensely as he did at so many levels while in London, yet also in the setting of a society so much more relaxed, open and tolerant as was England compared with Germany just then, he would not have been induced to continue his reflections on the Sermon on the Mount – reflections that were to ignite powerfully two years later in his teaching and writing on *Discipleship.*

Bonhoeffer's choice to move to London in the autumn of 1933 has to be seen against his own life and developments in Germany over the two years since the World Alliance Conference in Cambridge. It was a time of extraordinarily intense activity. He was ordained in November 1931. He launched into lecturing in the University of Berlin, his courses dealing with history of systematic theology, creation and sin, and Christology. He became student chaplain at the Charlottenburg technical college. He took charge of a boys' confirmation class in the working-class district of Berlin-Wedding. And he threw himself into his work as a youth secretary for the World Alliance. This work brought him to England again, to a meeting of the youth committee combined with an Anglo-French youth conference, in Epsom, April 1932. It also led him to organizing study conferences in Germany, France and Czechoslovakia, in which he attacked vigorously the rising nationalist theology of "orders of creation" (race, nation etc) that he saw as providing the justification for war. As an official of the World Alliance he attended its executive committee in Geneva in August 1932, and took part in the notable joint conference of the World Alliance and Life and Work at nearby Gland a few days later. Through his World Alliance committee work, as well as coming to know Bishop Arthur Burroughs, Bonhoeffer was developing relations with a wider circle of British collaborators, such as J.C. Bacon, H.W. Fox and R.E. Burlingham. But at Geneva and Gland he also for

Charles Freer Andrews

the first time encountered one of the most extraordinary British figures on the international church scene – Charles Freer Andrews. An Anglican priest, Andrews (1871-1940) had spent most of his life in India and inculturated himself deeply into the Indian scene, becoming a leader in the ashram of Rabindranath Tagore and a friend and supporter of Mahatma Gandhi. Deeply committed to identification with the poor and to peace and non-violence he had moved close to Quaker belief and practice, but in later years was to resume his regular Anglican priestly vocation. Bonhoeffer, already interested in India and the practice of non-violence, had his eye on him from the start.

Hitler broadcasts to the people, January 1933

Adolf Hitler came to power on 30 January 1933. "This means war," said Hans von Dohnanyi, Dietrich Bonhoeffer's brother-in-law, who was a civil servant in the ministry of justice. It was a sentiment shared by the whole family who regarded the nationalist revolutionary ferment with disgust, most notably the boycott of Jewish shops in April that year. The churches too were caught up in the ferment, with calls for the Protestant church to "conform" to the new National Socialist order. The demands were led by the so-called "Faith Movement of German Christians" (*Deutsche Christen*) who were advocating the primacy of race and nationhood in the created order, the imposition of the "leadership-principle" into government of the church, and the exclusion of all "non-Aryan" (i.e. of Jewish descent) pastors from church office: a truly German church for the German people, "completing the work of Martin Luther", it was claimed. There followed a tumultuous summer for the churches. Hitler appointed Ludwig Müller, a previous nonentity but a devoted Nazi and former naval chaplain, to be his plenipotentiary in church affairs and

Martin Niemöller

to bring about the unification of Protestantism in one Reich church. The bullying tactics of the "German Christians" (who had their own uniforms akin to the "Brownshirt" storm-troopers) combined with Müller's varying between heavy-handedness and serpentine evasiveness provoked huge opposition, much of it grouped around Martin Niemöller, a former U-boat captain, now pastor and lively preacher in the fashionable Dahlem church in Berlin. But things grew worse with the campaign of lying and intimidation that led to the resignation of the saintly Friedrich von Bodelschwingh as first "Reich bishop" and his replacement by Ludwig Müller, the rigged church elections in July that led to a German Christian victory, and the way the synod of the Prussian Church was effectively manhandled into capture by the German Christians – the so-called "Brown Synod". In response, in September Martin Niemöller formed the Pastors' Emergency League that quickly had 6,000 members, a good number of whom soon found themselves in prison.

Bonhoeffer, together with a group of loyal students he had attracted through his classes, was deeply involved in the turmoil on behalf of the opposition to the German Christians. For him the central issue was stark and clear: a church that allowed a racial principle (the so-called "Aryan-clause") to determine its membership, and that brought political principles into its governance, was no longer the church of Jesus Christ and could no longer claim to be the historic Evangelical Church of Germany, founded upon the scriptures and the confessions of the Reformation. He debated the issues in public, even with such eminent opponents as the theologian Emmanuel Hirsch. Through the summer he worked on a new confession designed to meet the challenge of the hour – the "Bethel Confession" so-called because it was largely worked on at the Bethel institute for the handicapped near Bielefeld, led by Friedrich von Bodelschwingh. He was grieved that once it got into the hands of cautious church leaders the text of the confession was largely gutted of its prophetic content. Just prior to the church elections he and his companion Gerhard Jacobi nearly got themselves arrested by the Gestapo for their leaflet campaign on behalf of their "Gospel and Church" group. With his friend Franz Hildebrandt, Martin Niemöller's assistant at Dahlem and a "non-Aryan", Bonhoeffer also conducted a pamphlet war against the policy of Müller at the National Synod that took place at Wittenberg in September.

By this time Bonhoeffer felt battle-fatigued. The theological issues to him were clear but he was increasingly uncertain how they should be fought. Long-standing friendships were cracking under the strain of theological dispute and ecclesiastical in-fighting. He felt increasingly isolated, even from people he highly respected, and was not sure how far his own judgement was to be trusted. In short, he wanted a break, a place where he could find himself again before returning to the fray. He had always wanted to be a pastor as well as a teacher and now the opportunity presented itself of being minister to the German congregation in Sydenham, London. He took advice from friends both in Germany and England, including Arthur Burroughs who suggested to him that Britain needed just such an interpreter of Germany at that moment. In July he preached a trial sermon at Sydenham and the congregation warmly invited him to come. There followed some tense discussions with Ludwig Müller and the Church External Affairs office who were suspicious of Bonhoeffer on account of his radicalism and his ecumenical activities. But he insisted that he was entitled to go due to the clear call of the congregation and having been given leave of absence by the university – but also made it clear that he would not be representing the "German Christian" position abroad. The one tie that might have kept him in Germany at this time was his engagement to Elisabeth Zinn, a cousin twice removed who was herself a theologian.

Arrival in London

On 17 October 1933 Dietrich Bonhoeffer arrived at 23 Manor Mount, Forest Hill in south-east London. The manse was – and still is – a huge double-fronted three-storey Victorian house that today displays a "blue plaque" recording the fact of Bonhoeffer's eighteen month residence. At that time part of it was occupied by a private school but even so there was still more than enough room for a single pastor and his housekeeper. It was also damp and

The manse, 23 Manor Mount, Forest Hill

Forest Hill, Cobb's Corner (around 1930)

draughty, heated only by a gas-fire in each room, and continually invaded by mice. The prospect was better outside, for Forest Hill indeed lives up to its name and from Manor Mount (on a clear day) there are fine views south to Kent and Surrey and northwards across London as far as Hampstead Heath. Forest Hill is a largely residential area, born out of the southward extension of the railway in the mid-nineteenth century. Sydenham has much older origins but like Forest Hill became part of the southward spread of suburbia, though perhaps with more upmarket housing than its younger neighbour. Both districts are now within the borough of Lewisham and many people would be hard put to tell where one ends and the other begins. But they do still each have their own railway station, about a mile apart.

In 1933 there were six German expatriate Protestant congregations (not including a Methodist one) in London. St George's, Sydenham, belonged to the United tradition (that is, embracing both the Lutheran and Reformed confessions). The building dated from 1875 and stood in Dacres Road, close to the railway line about midway between the Forest Hill and Sydenham stations (some would say that technically it lay within Forest Hill but that most of the congregation lived in Sydenham),

St George's German Church, Sydenham

about fifteen minutes' walk from the manse. Relatively affluent, reflecting the ambience of Sydenham, its members included diplomats, prosperous merchants and business people. Sunday attendance averaged 30-40.

Over some years of financial constraint, however, St George's had shared its pastor with another congregation, the St Paul's German Reformed Church in London's East End. This community had a history dating back to the early 18th century. Its present building was in Goulston Street, close by Aldgate tube station. The congregation was a somewhat different social mix to Sydenham: tradespeople, small shopkeepers and the like. There had been much intermarriage with the

St Paul's church, Aldgate

native population over the generations, and English was for many of the community now the first or only language. Bonhoeffer would often preach here in English. Attendance averaged about 50 and the church boasted a fine choir directed by Mr E.A. Seymour, a Fellow of the Royal College of Organists, no less. With a more informal atmosphere than Sydenham, its close-knit circle of interrelated families, its social life built around the choir, its outings and picnics, it had much of the ambience of a typical English free church of the time.

These two communities comprised the flock Bonhoeffer was to pastor for the next year and a half. The previous incumbent, Friedrich Singer, had just retired to his native Swabia after eight years' kindly but uneventful ministry in London, and in Bonhoeffer's eyes the congregations were in "a somewhat neglected state". That might pass as the presumptuous attitude of many a new (and young) pastor, but St George's and St Paul's were to experience remarkably concentrated attention from their pastor in the coming months, all his wider activities notwithstanding. On his first Sunday in the pulpit at Sydenham, 22 October – that day of curious hopes, expectations and anxieties on the part of a congregation – Bonhoeffer gave a clear foretaste of what was to come in a bold and uncompromising sermon on 2 Corinthians 5:20: "So we are ambassadors for Christ, God making his appeal through us. We beseech you on behalf of Christ, be reconciled to God." A change in pastors matters less than continuity in the preaching of the gospel, which is all that really counts in the life of the church. Why does the church seem so dull, so occupied with trivia? *"It is because we prefer quiet and edification to the holy restlessness of the powerful Lord God, because we keep thinking we have God in our power instead of allowing God to have power over us . . . It is because we like too much to talk and think about a cosy, comfortable God instead of letting ourselves be disturbed and disquieted by the presence of God – because in the end we ourselves do not want to believe that God is really right here among us, right now, demanding that we hand ourselves over, in life and death, in heart and soul and body."* After the opening formalities at his first meetings with the congregational councils of both St George's and St Paul's, he immediately launched into a discussion of how to increase youth participation in the life of the churches, starting a Sunday school, having a nativity play and special services events organized for Christmas, and so on. A few weeks later when the German pastors from all over England met together in Bradford (see below, page 37) each was asked to say in five minutes what had been happening in his church. Bonhoeffer's comment was that five minutes was far too long to describe what he had done so far, but if it was a matter of what he was planning and hoping to do it would be far too short! His call to the pastorate was soon ratified by congregational assemblies of both churches.

Bonhoeffer quickly made London his home. In this he was aided by another recent German arrival in the city, Julius Rieger, who earlier that year had come to be pastor of the St George's Lutheran Church in Whitechapel (not too far from Bonhoeffer's St Paul's Church) and chaplain to the German Seamen's Mission. Five years older than Bonhoeffer, he had been on the staff of the Preachers' Seminary in Naumberg. Although he and his wife Johanna had attended the World Alliance conference in Cambridge in 1931 as visitors, and he knew of some of Bonhoeffer's theological works, before Bonhoeffer's arrival in London their acquaintance was slight. They soon developed a strong friendship, as often is the case when people of similar age and background find themselves together in

Julius Rieger

a foreign environment. Frequently they telephoned each other as the weekend approached for mutual advice on the Sunday sermon. Rieger kept a diary and many of his entries reveal just how fully Bonhoeffer shared with him news and information

Dr Barnardo's village for children, Barkingside

(some very confidential) from the unfolding saga in Berlin. Moreover, together they "did" London. Some of their visits aimed to increase their knowledge of English social and pastoral work, as when they spent some hours at Dr Barnardo's "village" for children at Barkingside. But as often as not they went out for sheer pleasure. Both were avid cinema-goers, with a predilection for spine-chilling thrillers. Not only in theology but also in food their tastes were similar. Often they ate together in Schmidt's restaurant in Charlotte Street or met for tea in the New Criterion. Bonhoeffer particularly relished oriental dishes and so the Shanghai restaurant in Greek Street, Soho and the Burma restaurant near Charing Cross station were favourite resorts. They explored the treasures of the British Museum together. When six years later Bonhoeffer's twin-sister Sabine and her family were living as refugees in London, Sabine discovered how Dietrich during his visit with them was able to conduct them around like a native: Buckingham Palace, St Paul's Cathedral, the Tower, Kew Gardens, Hampton Court . . . and much else. But the place he always revelled in above all was the National Gallery, on Trafalgar Square.

Trafalgar Square and the National Gallery

Perhaps somewhat surprisingly, Bonhoeffer seems to have spent very little if any time in the concert-halls of London. But there was no lack of music in the Sydenham manse. His Bechstein piano had been shipped from Berlin. There was constant music-making, especially as so many of his guests and visitors, who included former students from Berlin, were musically or vocally able. There were choir rehearsals for the church (with some difficulty, he got a choir started at St George's). There was the gramophone. Impressed by the sound of English choirs, he bought the whole set of a recent recording of the Bach *Mass in B-Minor*.

Continental jokes about the English are mostly about their food. Whatever else, Bonhoeffer highly approved of the traditional English breakfast which, by all accounts, in the Sydenham manse was a sumptuous affair eaten about mid-morning. (The actual domestic arrangements in the manse remain somewhat unclear. There is one account of a housekeeper whom Bonhoeffer described as suffering from "religious dementia" and who had to be dismissed because the kitchen was sinking into chaos. Another story is that a female acquaintance from Germany came to keep house for him but was relieved of her duties when it became evident that her attentions to the pastor were liable to exceed those for which she was being paid. Possibly these are variants of the same story.) Facing the challenge of his first

English Christmas, he was invited to the dinner table of Lawrence Whitburn and his wife, members of the Sydenham church. An enormous turkey arrived on the table and no-one, not even Whitburn himself, had the nerve to start carving. "Whilst we all held the unfortunate bird down, otherwise it would have landed on the carpet, Bonhoeffer went into the attack with the carving knife. We all fed fully and richly, but my wife and I will never forget the sight of that dissected skeleton. As we often remarked later – Bonhoeffer was capable of anything."

One thing Bonhoeffer was not capable of, however, was surviving the English winter, its fog – in those coal-fired days a real menace in London – and the damp and draughts at Manor Mount, without succumbing to bouts of colds and 'flu. But the English spring was a revelation to him. In May 1934 he wrote his grandmother, Julie Bonhoeffer, a touching account of a day outing with the St Paul's Church to Epping Forest, on the north-east edge of London (and in those days a favourite for excursions out of the grimy city for churches and Sunday schools, particularly as they were deliberately catered for with non-alcoholic bars and cafés there). He tells her:

> Just now it's quite lovely here. We had a church excursion yesterday and were outdoors all day, in an area that is famous because at this time of year the whole forest floor is absolutely covered in blue, for hundreds of metres, by a kind of bell-flower. Furthermore, I was greatly surprised to find wild rhododendrons just coming into bloom, and probably in two weeks they will be a fabulous sight. It's a completely different climate here, very unpleasant in winter, but that much more beautiful in spring.

The flower was of course the bluebell, hitherto unknown to Bonhoeffer since *Endymion non-scriptus* while a familiar springtime sight in Britain is very rare on the continent. There was probably another reason why Epping Forest appealed to him. When he saw the English Lake District on one of his northward journeys with Julius Rieger he confessed himself slightly disappointed. He could not deny the grandeur of mountain and lake but the relatively treeless landscape made him long even more for the rolling woods and forests of his beloved Harz mountains, the summer holiday haunt of the Bonhoeffer family for as long as he could remember.

This then was the English setting in which Bonhoeffer lived and worked, and from which he drew enjoyment and inspiration, while in London. It needs to be kept in mind that there was always this counterpart to the tensions, confrontations and struggles that beset him day by day.

Karl Barth and three wise men

Almost the first thing that Dietrich Bonhoeffer did on arrival in Forest Hill was to pen a long, handwritten letter to Karl Barth explaining his decision to leave Germany for a spell in England at such a critical time for the German church. It is a letter of soul-baring, about the uncertainties and growing sense of isolation that had beset him in recent months, and his deeply felt need to go for a time into the wilderness before returning to the fray – and his long-standing wish to be a pastor. Barth's reply was a thunderous, crashing broadside. What on earth was Bonhoeffer up to, deserting the field of battle at this time? What did he imagine he could do for the cause from across the English Channel? Why this wish to play Elijah under the juniper tree or Jonah under the gourd? Get back to your machine-gun post like a good soldier! "Just be glad I don't have you here in front of me, because then I'd find another whole way of putting it to you forcefully that you need to drop all these quirks and special considerations, however fascinating, and just think of one thing: that you are a German, that your church's house is on fire, and in fact you ought to return to your post by the next ship! Well, let's say the next but one. But I cannot tell you expressly and urgently enough that you belong in Berlin and not in London."

Bonhoeffer was sufficiently unnerved by this riposte to send it to his father for comment. Karl Bonhoeffer opined that it showed a lively spirit – but also that to stand outside the immediate situation, as Dietrich was doing, might have real benefits in the long-term. In fact for incidental reasons Barth's letter did not reach Bonhoeffer until late November. Had it arrived by return of post who can tell what Bonhoeffer's reaction might have been? As it happens, in the course of those intervening weeks it was becoming confirmed to Bonhoeffer that, *pace* Barth (who was only just beginning to appreciate the significance of the ecumenical world), for the moment he did belong in London as well as in Berlin. Crucial to this realization was the formation of relationships with key actors on the British scene. Three persons in particular must be highlighted.

The first is Baron Bruno Schröder (1867-1940), who was president of the Association of German Evangelical Congregations in Great Britain and Ireland and a leading merchant banker. He was born in Hamburg and came to London in 1893 to work in his uncle's bank, J. Henry Schröder and Co., soon afterwards becoming a partner in the firm and then senior partner, effectively managing it for the next four decades. With the outbreak of war in 1914 Bruno Schröder applied for and was given

Baron Bruno Schröder

naturalization as a British citizen. His ties with his native Germany remained strong for the rest of his life, and as a loyal Protestant (a member of the German Christchurch congregation in London) and of considerable social standing in both Britain and Germany, he admirably filled the role of presiding over the general affairs of the German congregations in the British Isles. At the time of Bonhoeffer's arrival in London the post of secretary of the Association of Congregations was vacant and Bonhoeffer had been recommended to Schröder as a suitable candidate (in fact he declined the invitation on the grounds of his inexperience in England, the post being taken instead by another London pastor, Fritz Wehran). The two were in contact almost as soon as Bonhoeffer landed in London, and very shortly thereafter Bonhoeffer was presenting his credentials at Schröder's office in the City. Theirs was to be a somewhat formal but highly important relationship of mutual trust and respect, and Schröder's support for Bonhoeffer and his like-minded colleagues in their disputes with the Reich church authorities in Berlin was to be rock-solid. In appearance and bearing he appeared the epitome of the successful Prussian aristocrat, and if he was conservative by disposition, with no pretences to be a theologian, he also knew what was – and was not – fair play. While he had some initial sympathy with what looked like the revival of German national morale in the early 1930s he had no truck with the Nazis once they were in power, and the story became current how one day he literally threw the German ambassador to London, Joachim von Ribbentrop, out of his office.

The second, and arguably *the* key figure, is Bishop George Bell. In 1933 Bell, then aged 48, had been bishop of Chichester for four years after an already distinguished

George Bell, Bishop of Chichester

career including ten years as chaplain to Randall Davidson, archbishop of Canterbury, followed by five years as dean of Canterbury Cathedral. He was now completing his monumental, two-volume biography of Randall Davidson (published in 1935), which virtually constitutes a history of the Church of England in the first quarter of the 20th century. Bell was passionately interested in the performing arts, and had no mean gifts himself as shown by the award to him of a major poetry prize while an undergraduate at Oxford. (Today, his most familiar legacy in verse is his hymn on Christian unity *Christ is the king! O friends rejoice*, remarkable in its time not least because of the extent of its gender-inclusive language.) At Canterbury he brought religious drama into the cathedral, commissioning works by contemporary writers, the most enduringly famous of which is T.S. Eliot's *Murder in the Cathedral*. At Chichester, Bell was to encourage the same interests throughout his diocese.

Bell represented the more broad-minded catholic tendency in the Church of England, and from his time as archbishop's chaplain he was deeply committed both to the search for Christian unity and to the reconciling mission of the church in the world. He was not an exceptionally profound scholar or original thinker, but he studied widely and assiduously and had the capacity to see into the heart of an issue and to communicate his convictions cogently and persistently. He was also gifted in developing relationships of patent sincerity with figures from other traditions, and was a superbly firm but gentle diplomat at the conference table. He had attended the 1925 Stockholm Conference on Life and Work (and spoke powerfully on the need for a strong continuing organization), and a number of other ecumenical encounters in Europe. In 1932, following the death of Theodore Woods, Bishop of Winchester, he was elected President of the Universal Christian Council for Life and Work. He and Dietrich Bonhoeffer were therefore together in Geneva at the ecumenical meetings taking place in August that year, but that did not constitute their first real encounter. Bell at that point saw Bonhoeffer – if at all – as just another young German present for the World Alliance committee. Bonhoeffer, for his part, had already had indirect dealings with Bell when he oversaw the translation into German of Bell's booklet *A Brief Sketch of the Church of England* on behalf of the World Alliance.

Matters changed rapidly on Bonhoeffer's arrival in England. By then it was clear that with the dramatic turn of events in Germany, and especially the Church Struggle, George Bell could play a key role as occupant of one of the leading positions in the ecumenical movement as it then existed. Bonhoeffer was very interested in the possibility of meeting him and brought with him a letter of introduction from Adolf Deissmann, professor of New Testament in Berlin and a leading figure in the World Alliance from its outset. Meanwhile Bell had received directly a similarly warm commendation of Bonhoeffer from H.L. Henriod, the secretary of both Life and Work and the World Alliance in Geneva. The stage was therefore well set for the first Bell-Bonhoeffer encounter early in November, when the executive committees of Life and Work and the World Alliance met in London. Bonhoeffer enjoyed meeting such English colleagues as Arthur Burroughs, Tom Craske and H.W. Fox again, and on their home territory. But the prize encounter was with George Bell who invited him to lunch at that most patrician of London clubs, the Athenaeum on Pall Mall.

Each recognized the importance of the other: in Bell Bonhoeffer saw someone who, in sympathy with the church opposition in Germany, could do so much to rally opinion on its behalf throughout the ecumenical world; in Bonhoeffer, Bell (who spoke hardly any German) saw someone uniquely placed both to inform him about and to interpret what was going on in Germany.

The Athenaeum, Pall Mall, London

There soon followed an invitation for Bonhoeffer to spend a couple of days at Chichester, which Bonhoeffer accepted gladly though with a little wariness as to the etiquette involved in being entertained by an English bishop (should he bring a dinner-jacket?). On 21 November he caught an afternoon train from Victoria station and was met at Brighton by Bell's chaplain Lancelot Mason who took him to the diocesan Church House, where the bishop emerged from a committee to take tea with his visitor. Then, with Mason at the wheel they drove west to Chichester and as the car rolled between the Sussex Downs and the sea they resumed in earnest their discussion about the German church scene. Chichester itself was a delight

Chichester Cathedral and Palace today

Mrs Henrietta Bell

to Bonhoeffer. Never too high-minded to despise the enjoyments of gracious living he revelled in the relaxed spaciousness of the bishop's palace and the Bells' generous hospitality, which enabled the further examination of the theological and political issues at stake in Germany to become, if not pleasurable, then at least satisfying business. For their part the Bells were thrilled to have such a guest who, as well as being from a background new to them, enjoyed a fine wine and made such good conversation at the dinner-table. Years later on BBC radio Henrietta Bell recalled: "I remember him very clearly. He was an exceptionally attractive, vigorous, lively man with plenty of rather unruly chestnut hair and bright, eager blue eyes. And I remember after he left saying, 'Well, that really was a very unusually attractive person.'"

So began what was to become one of the most significant Christian friendships of the 20th century. In some ways Bell and Bonhoeffer were contrasting figures: Bell the sagacious, broadminded catholic Anglican, Bonhoeffer the Barthian radical. There was also the difference in age – Bell was almost if not quite old enough to be Bonhoeffer's father, but that disparity became a positive factor in the relationship. Bell was soon to be calling Bonhoeffer and his friend Franz Hildebrandt "my boys" and that may indicate a deeper emotional note being rung on his side, for the Bells were childless. Bonhoeffer, for his part, for all his strength of character and independence of mind did at times feel the need for counsel older and wiser than his own. His father, Karl Barth and now George Bell were to be the only people to whom he really accorded this role. There were other factors that Bell and Bonhoeffer found they had in common: they shared the same birthday (4 February); for each, the First World War had taken brothers – in Bell's case, two. But in the coming years of struggle and conflict in the church and the world they were to prove to one another that "there is a friend that sticketh closer than a brother" (Proverbs 18:24). In 1942 the friendship was to culminate in a dramatic and poignant venture of ecumenical solidarity in resistance to tyranny.

The third figure is the Scottish lay theologian and ecumenical worker J.H. Oldham. "Joe" Oldham was secretary of the International Missionary Council (IMC), but that job-title is hopelessly inadequate to indicate the vast range of interests and activities that he directed from his desk at Edinburgh House, Eaton Gate. One might almost say he *was* the ecumenical movement. He was born in 1874 and at Oxford his Christian commitment was nurtured in the student evangelical and missionary movement. After a few years as a YMCA missionary volunteer in India (the land of his birth) he studied theology at Edinburgh and in Halle, Germany. John R. Mott, the formidably dynamic leader of the worldwide student missionary movement, recruited him as organizing secretary for the 1910

J.H. Oldham

World Missionary Conference at Edinburgh, generally recognized as the birth of the modern ecumenical movement, and afterwards Oldham continued as full-time secretary of the conference's Continuation Committee – the first permanent, international ecumenical structure. Oldham founded and for over twenty years edited the quarterly *International Review of Missions*, which for a long time was the only journal of the ecumenical movement at world level. The nationalist bitterness of the First World War almost completely shattered the relations that had been built at Edinburgh (and in the World Alliance) between the German church and missionary leaders on the one hand, and their British, American and French counterparts on the other. That reconciliation did take place afterwards, and relatively quickly, owed much to initiatives quietly undertaken by Oldham. During the war itself, he was instrumental in preventing the British government confiscating the property of the German missions in British territories or in countries now occupied by the British. Moreover, it was he who saw to it that the Versailles Treaty, so severe in other ways, included a clause that was to ensure the right of the Germans to resume their missionary work in all areas. These must count among the most remarkable and effective examples ever of Christian reconciliation. At first, during and immediately after the bitterness of war, the Germans did not appreciate what Oldham had done. But when they did, they never forgot it and no one in Britain during the 1920s and 1930s was more highly regarded among the ecumenically minded Germans than he. (It might be added that when, years after his death in 1969, work was launched on the biography of Oldham, it was the German churches that largely funded the research and writing.)

In 1921 the International Missionary Council, the truly permanent if long-awaited child of Edinburgh 1910, was formed with Oldham as its secretary. From the start Oldham wished the IMC agenda to embrace education, social justice and international relations as much as evangelism in the traditional sense. Much of his attention throughout the 1920s focused on Africa. He mobilized church opinion in defence of African rights in Kenya, persuaded British colonial policy to include adequate research on African problems, encouraged greater partnership in African education between government and missions, and co-founded the International Institute of African Languages and Cultures. Written in the midst of all this engagement was his most substantial book in a lifetime of prolific writing, *Christianity and the Race Problem* (1924), a pioneering and prophetic work that still stands as a classic of Christian social ethics – followed next year by his tiny but hugely popular, *A Devotional Diary,* used for daily prayer and meditation by thousands of people until well after the Second World War. It was this blend of study, political acumen and personal piety that earned Oldham the description "a wily saint". Probably apocryphal, but certainly true to character, is the motto attributed to him: "Find out where power lies and then take it to lunch at the Athenaeum" – for, like Bell, he too was a member of that prestigious establishment. He had built up an enormous network of contacts: archbishops, other clergy of all ranks and denominations, academics (from Oxford to Harvard), scientists, anthropologists, educationists, government ministers, civil servants in the Colonial Office, colonial governors, ambassadors and other diplomats, newspaper editors . . . and many more.

By the early 1930s, conscious of the developing crises on the continent, Oldham was turning his mind to Europe again and not least Germany. Ever a voracious reader, he was well abreast of the newer developments in theology and philosophy, becoming decidedly sympathetic to the "theology of crisis", and moreover knew such as Karl Barth, Emil Brunner and Eberhard Grisebach personally. Even, in 1932, he obtained and read Dietrich Bonhoeffer's *Akt und Sein* – at least a full year before they actually met. In Oldham, therefore, Bonhoeffer had a resource in London who knew German and Germany better than any other church-related official of the time. They were to meet a number of times, probably both at the Athenaeum and at Edinburgh House but equally likely also at Oldham's home, the Dial House at Chipstead in Surrey, where Joe and his wife Mary were famously hospitable to guests from all over the world. At the practical level Oldham was to be especially helpful to Bonhoeffer over finding assistance for refugees from Germany and no less, though not on such a public level than Bell, in securing ecumenical support for the church opposition in Germany. Between them Bonhoeffer, Bell and Oldham made a diverse but effective team. They were to be together at the crucial conference at Fanø, Denmark, in August 1934.

Both Bell and Oldham were to do much more for the ecumenical movement in the coming years, not least in the formation and leadership of the World Council of Churches. Both are commemorated in the Ecumenical Centre in Geneva – Bell by a meeting room named after him, and Oldham by a sundial bearing the tribute "Missionary Statesman, Foremost Pioneer of WCC, Friend of Africa". The late Adrian Hastings in his survey of English Christianity in the 20th century proposes Dietrich Bonhoeffer as the greatest German, and George Bell as the greatest British, Christian of the time. If we are to indulge in such invidious human judgments, then on the British side Joe Oldham also has a claim to have his hat in the ring. It is probably better not to adjudicate at all, but for our purposes simply to note that during his last weeks in London in 1935 before returning to Germany, Bonhoeffer wrote letters of warm personal thanks to just these three people: Baron Schröder, George Bell and Joe Oldham.

The Church Struggle – waged from London

If anyone – Karl Barth or even Bonhoeffer himself – thought that by coming to London Bonhoeffer would be opting out of the Church Struggle being waged in Germany, they were colossally mistaken. Having got to London, for all the uncertainties that had prompted him to leave Germany he found his heart was still in the conflict back home. It was not just that he wanted to know what was going on. Many people in Berlin already wanted to keep him up to the mark: colleagues in the ministry such as Franz Hildebrandt and Gerhard Jacobi, former students, and not least his mother, Paula Bonhoeffer, who, as a keen admirer of Martin Niemöller, kept her ear close to the ground and was often amazingly well-informed. Letters and telegrams flew to and fro, not to mention lengthy telephone calls. Not all popular anecdotes about Bonhoeffer are verifiable, but the story that his telephone bill became so hugely unpayable that eventually the Forest Hill Post Office gave him special dispensation, is actually true.

Bonhoeffer's London-based engagement in the conflict was on three distinct but closely related fronts: (1) his efforts to influence directly the course of events in Germany through entreaty or advice to his allies there; (2) his bringing of the other German pastors and congregations in Britain to side with the church opposition and eventually the Confessing Church; (3) his recruitment of the ecumenical movement into the struggle.

On the first front Bonhoeffer was not left on his own for every long, for in November he was joined by Franz Hildebrandt, his friend since 1927, who stayed with him in the Sydenham manse for several weeks until early in the New Year. Hildebrandt as a "non-Aryan" was in an increasingly difficult position as a pastor alongside Niemöller in Dahlem. On 13 November, just two days after Hildebrandt's arrival, there occurred in Berlin one of the most grotesque events in the whole church saga, when the German Christians held a massive rally in the Berlin Sports Palace. Dr Reinhard Krause, leader of the Berlin Nazi party not only called for immediate implementation of the Aryan clause in the church but for "liberation from the Old Testament with its Jewish money morality and from these stories of cattle dealers and pimps." Even some "moderate" German Christians were scandalized. More worrying was the fact that official representatives of the Reich church who were present had said nothing in protest. Seen from England the prospects were now very ambiguous for a concerted opposition. On the one hand the Sports Palace event was so disgraceful that it could lead to the complete and final discrediting both of the German Christians and of their vain and incompetent patron Reich bishop Müller. On the other hand, a discredited enemy does not ipso facto mean a vindicated and victorious opposition, and Bonhoeffer and Hildebrandt were continually worried about the stance of the friends in Berlin. Would they really stand fast on *theological* and not just church-political grounds in opposition to those substituting race and ideology for Christ and the gospel? What about the rumoursof splits in the opposition even between Niemöller and Jacobi? Would they be tempted by offers of high position in the Reich church government? Could the southern German Lutheran bishops really be relied upon to stand firm with the rest of German Protestantism? And so on. The wires between London and Berlin rang very hot at times during those weeks. The news got even grimmer. In December Müller declared the Protestant youth organizations incorporated into the Hitler Youth, and soon after issued a decree – "The Muzzling Decree" in the words of the opposition – forbidding any public or pulpit discussion about the church situation.

On the second front, that of the other German pastors and congregations in England, Bonhoeffer made considerable progress. As well as the six London parishes there were German congregations with pastors in Bradford, Hull, Liverpool, Manchester, South Shields and Newcastle-upon-Tyne – a distinctly northern constituency. The pastors varied considerably in age, theological background and political inclination. Not all were like Julius Rieger. Gustav Schönberger, for example, pastor of the Hamburg Lutheran Church in Dalston, London, was actually a National Socialist party member, though that did not prevent him siding with Bonhoeffer in support of the Confessing Church on strictly theological grounds. (If this seems surprising, it must be recognized that during the days before and just after the coming of the Third Reich Nazism had a considerable following among people who still saw it, despite certain "excesses", as an idealistic movement restoring honour and moral purpose to Germany and a bulwark against communism. Among them, for a time, were even such as Martin Niemöller.)

Bonhoeffer's chance to meet all his English-based German colleagues (those in London met frequently among themselves) came a little over a month after his arrival in London, as the annual conference of the pastors was to take place 27-30 November in Bradford, Yorkshire. So, less than a week after sampling the south coast breezes and historic gentility of Chichester, Bonhoeffer headed north for his first encounter with industrial England and the chimney-forests of the woollen mills. Bonhoeffer and Rieger shared a room in a somewhat spartan hotel. The meetings took place in the German Church in Great Horton Road, just south-west of the centre of Bradford, hosted by the pastor Wilhelm Hansen. The congregation

The German Church, Bradford

comprised all sections of Bradford society, from the urban poor to those whom wool had made successful and prosperous. There was an evening session joined by the whole congregation. Talks were given on ministry in an environment where male unemployment stood at over 13 per cent and housing conditions for many were wretched. The pastors shared news and information on their parish work. Bonhoeffer gave a theological lecture on ministry and preaching.

One afternoon the pastors went by bus to York, to admire the Minster and to meet the dean, H.N. Bate who invited them all to tea. Bate himself had good contacts with Germany and had had at least one pastor from Germany as a guest worker with him. But Bonhoeffer, according to Rieger, seemed uninterested and detached from this occasion although on the bus he had been deep in animated conversation with Karl-Heinz Schreiner of Liverpool. Maybe the deanery tea compared unfavourably with that in the palace at Chichester. Maybe he was just tired. More likely he was preoccupied with how to bring home to these pastors the real urgency of what was happening back in Germany. That opportunity presented itself, however, back in Bradford. The home scene was clearly going to take over the agenda, and people were eager to hear Bonhoeffer's first-hand and up to date news. He described in great detail the events of the of summer that he had witnessed and been involved in, including a vivid account of the notorious "Brown Synod" in Berlin, 5-6 September and the National Synod in Wittenberg on 27 September (Bonhoeffer had listened in from above the false ceiling), the growth of the opposition under Niemöller and Jacobi and the formation of the Pastors' Emergency League. But Bonhoeffer stressed the *theological* issues that were at stake: Müller was saying that at Judgment Day God would only ask a man if he had been a decent fellow and had served his country well. The cross was becoming merely a symbol for "public interest" over self-interest. The spirit of National Socialism, not the Holy Spirit, was being seen as the renewing power of the church. The Reformation faith was being eviscerated. German paganism was flaring up again.

The pastors were not just interested but alarmed and began to stir up enthusiasm for protest. A statement was drafted to be sent to the Reich church government warning that if such tendencies continued the close tie between their congregations and the mother church in Germany would be broken. This was the first clear warning to be issued from Britain. After Bradford the London pastors among themselves asked Baron Schröder to send an even sharper statement to Berlin – which he did, pointing out that the statutes of the congregations in Britain "give us full liberty to resign from the Church Federation should we so desire." If not a threat this was at least, in sporting terms, a yellow card. Meanwhile back in London, Bonhoeffer and Hildebrandt had both persuaded their colleagues in England to join Niemöller's Pastors' Emergency League and renewed their own campaign on Berlin, advocating that the German Christians, Müller and all his cohorts should be subjected to heresy trials and disciplined or else barred from entry into a completely new church order.

At Bradford, his relative youthfulness notwithstanding, Bonhoeffer had clearly made his mark in leading a growing protest movement in the German diaspora. Something else had happened there, more accurately somewhere on the road between Bradford and York. Years later, Rieger commented to Bonhoeffer that he sensed a significant difference in style between his earlier theological writing and his later works – these seemed much more accessible (many of us would agree). Bonhoeffer concurred, and put it down to that conversation with Karl-Heinz Schreiner on the bus to York. Schreiner had enthused over the style of Adolf Schlatter, noted professor of systematic theology and New Testament at Tübingen whose lectures Bonhoeffer had attended during his year as a student there. Schreiner's comments triggered off in Bonhoeffer a new regard for one of his earliest mentors and Eberhard Bethge remarks that in his later years no writer other than Luther was more fully represented than Schlatter on Bonhoeffer's bookshelves. Inhabitants of Yorkshire, the English county where pride is taken in calling a spade a spade instead of an agricultural implement, might think it entirely appropriate that he had taken this lesson to heart on one of their buses.

The third front, that of ecumenical relations, occupied Bonhoeffer's mind almost from the moment he arrived in London. There was no choice about this, for just three days beforehand the national leader of the German Christians, Joachim Hossenfelder, had also appeared in the capital. Hossenfelder, aged only 34, was just then riding the crest of the wave of German Christian popularity and success and had even, in September, been appointed to the prestigious bishopric of Berlin-Brandenburg. Accompanied by Professor Karl Fezer of Tübingen he was now in England on a charm offensive, aiming to win not only general support in church circles for the new Germany and the new German Christian

Joachim Hossenfelder

church, but the particular prize of an attendance of Anglican bishops at the consecration of Ludwig Müller as Reich bishop, scheduled to take place in December in Berlin's cathedral. The visit was an abject failure. There was no reception at Lambeth Palace – having been briefed by George Bell, the archbishop, Cosmo Gordon Lang, was well aware of how such an occasion would be exploited by the Nazi propaganda. No official meeting with any representative church gathering, in fact scarcely more than a dinner given by the German ambassador at which Hossenfelder made an embarrassingly inept speech, took place. Nor could Hossenfelder even claim to have had any official invitation to England in the first place. It was Frank Buchman's Oxford Movement, at that time flirting strongly with Nazism, which had issued the invitation.

There was, however, one notable exception to the cold-shouldering of Hossenfelder. Arthur Cayley Headlam (1862-1947), bishop of Gloucester, gave him an interview from which the two bishops emerged with mutual admiration. Headlam was a figure of formidable learning in theology and early church history and his route to Gloucester had been via a fellowship of All Souls, Oxford, a professorship at King's College, London, and then the Regius Chair of Divinity at Oxford. But he was by turns to puzzle, embarrass and infuriate many of his colleagues and British church opinion at large over the coming years by his sympathy for Hitler's Germany, his support for the Reich church and his withering dismissal of the Confessing Church and, even during his imprisonment, of Martin Niemöller. That Headlam was not only chairman of the Church of England's

Arthur Cayley Headlam, Bishop of Gloucester, with his chaplain Edward Prichard

Council of Foreign Relations but also a leading figure in the Faith and Order movement did not make ecumenical responses to the German scene any easier.

Bonhoeffer, briefed by George Bell, fully reported on the Hossenfelder episode to his friends in Berlin who understandably had been anxious about its possible consequences. In fact there was not much cause to worry about British public opinion at this stage. The press, especially the *Times*, was covering the German church drama on an almost daily basis, and the weekly religious press was even more focused on the scene. Reactions were of alarm and disgust at the overt anti-Semitism of the German Christians and the heavy-handed police actions employed or condoned by Ludwig Müller. Of course the precise issues felt in Germany itself to be at stake were not always clearly recognized. Typical was the comment in the *Baptist Times* on 13 December 1933: "Protestantism has won the first round in the conflict with Hitlerism which threatened to destroy it as a Christian Church. All other parties in the Reich, racial, social, and political, have been destroyed; Protestantism alone has successfully resisted Hitler's dictatorship and survived in the struggle." But while this description may have been vastly over-simplistic and unwarrantably triumphalistic it clearly expressed where Christian sentiment in Britain lay, and the article's following sentences describing the German Christian programme of non-Aryan, Nordic religiosity were entirely accurate. For Bonhoeffer and the other London pastors, to be in this atmosphere where the gut reaction in the British churches was so overwhelmingly in sympathy with the German church opposition, was a major factor in encouraging their continuing attack on the Reich church leadership. Bell himself was taking a high-level ecumenical initiative in writing a letter of concern to Reich bishop Müller.

At Christmas 1933 Bell and Bonhoeffer exchanged greetings. These were more than seasonal pleasantries. Bonhoeffer replied to Bell's: "It means very much to me indeed to know that you are sharing all the time the sorrows and the troubles which the last year has brought to our church in Germany. So we do not stand alone, and whatever may occur to one member of the Church universal, we know that all the members suffer with it. This is a great comfort for all of us; and if God will turn back to our church sometime now or later, then we may be certain, that, if one member be honoured, all the members shall rejoice with it." Bell furthered showed his solidarity not only with a letter in the *Times* of 17 January 1934, drawing attention to the significance of the "Muzzling Decree" and Müller's patent breaches of faith, but with further direct approaches to Müller himself and even President Hindenburg. When the Pastors' Emergency League issued a proclamation urging pastors not to obey the "Muzzling Decree" the London pastors sent a telegram to the Reich church government identifying themselves with the statement and declaring the withdrawal of their confidence from the Reich bishop. This was followed up by a telegram in similar terms from Bruno Schröder. The "now or later" of which Bonhoeffer had spoken to Bell at Christmas still seemed a long way off during that first month of 1934, which was proving a traumatic one for the church opposition. The first moves began to be made by such as Karl Barth and Gerhard Jacobi to convene independent, free synods. Secession from the Reich church was a clearly growing possibility. The question was how much support there would be for it, how united would the opposition remain, and on what basis? On 25 January Hitler held a long-awaited reception for Protestant church leaders. Many had hoped that this would enable them to expose Müller as untrustworthy and indeed distrusted by the church leadership at large, a hopeless candidate for uniting and pacifying the churches. In fact the reverse happened. Thanks largely to an intervention by Reich Marshal Hermann Göring who marched into the meeting and portentously announced that there was now evidence of the dissident pastors receiving help – including money – from abroad, Hitler lost his temper and berated the company for their incompetence and disloyalty. When Niemöller tried to mollify Hitler by insisting on their loyalty to the German Reich and people Hitler snapped back: "Leave the German people to me; you stick to your sermons." The meeting closed with the pastors in disarray, and Müller's position strengthened by default. It emerged that Göring's remarks were based on some incidental remarks made by Niemöller and his secretary on the telephone earlier in the day, a phone that had obviously been tapped.

Bonhoeffer himself, when he heard the news from Berlin, clearly regarded the chancellery reception as a disaster – one more disaster in a darkening scene. On the previous Sunday, 21 January, he had preached at Sydenham on Jeremiah 20:7: *O Lord, you have enticed me, and I was enticed; you have overpowered me, and you have prevailed.* It is one of Bonhoeffer's most personally engaged sermons, where he becomes Jeremiah and Jeremiah becomes the pastor who is irresistibly caught up in a struggle for the truth of God without any guarantee of success or recognition. All such a person knows is the experience of being captured by God, not out of desire or choice but simply with the noose around the neck. "*This path will lead right down into the deepest situation of human powerlessness. The follower becomes a laughingstock, scorned and taken for a fool, but a fool who is extremely dangerous to people's peace and comfort, so that he or she must be beaten, locked up, tortured, if not put to death right away. That is exactly what became of this man Jeremiah, because he could not get away from God. He was accused of fantasizing, being stubborn, disturbing the peace and being an enemy of the people, as have those in every age until the present day who were seized and possessed by God – for whom God had become too strong.*" Today in Germany, says Bonhoeffer later in the sermon, thousands of parishioners and pastors are facing oppression and persecution because of their witness for the truth, forgoing peace and quiet under the divine compulsion.

Not to be able to get away from God is the constantly disquieting thing in the life of every Christian.

Ten years later, in prison, it will again be to Jeremiah that Bonhoeffer will return to find himself in the mirror of faith, when the text will be 45:5: "And you, do you seek great things for yourself? Do not seek them . . ." And it is hardly necessary to point out that in this sermon much of the imagery used to describe the fate of the persecuted prophet was to prove uncannily prophetic of the preacher himself . . . even to the point of the noose over his head.

From their own point of view, Bonhoeffer and his London colleagues must have felt relatively helpless to influence the course of events in Berlin, which now took an even more ominous turn as Müller sought to consolidate his accidental victory of 25 January: Niemöller was suspended from office (his place in the Dahlem pulpit however taken by Franz Hildebrandt, to great effect), and soon more than 50 more pastors suffered the same fate. The protests and declarations from London had had the effect of continual and accurate sniper fire on the Reich church administration, and in Berlin it was decided that a high-level task-force be dispatched to London to sort out this nest of dissidents. It was led by Theodor Heckel, *Oberkonsistorialrat* in the Reich church office with overall respon-

Theodor Heckel

sibility for relations between the mother church and German congregations abroad. Older than Bonhoeffer by twelve years, he and Bonhoeffer had had friendly relations at the start of the Church Struggle but as events unfolded it became clear that Heckel, who avowedly claimed a strict neutrality between the different parties, was in fact tacitly if not explicitly sympathetic to Müller and the German Christian cause. He and the church authorities were desperately anxious to keep the conflict out of the diaspora congregations, since any echoes abroad of trouble in Germany made further bad news for the Reich and the church alike. Already, the foreign press was far too interested in the church dispute and no more so than in Britain.

Heckel, accompanied by two church officials, visited London 8-9 February and had two lengthy sessions with the pastors. The meetings were tense and at times heated. With a mixture of legalistic pedantry, evasion as to the facts about outright persecution, thinly-veiled threats and (worst of all in Bonhoeffer's eyes) a total refusal to see the theological matter at the heart of the Church Struggle, Heckel sought to bring the pastors into line. Bonhoeffer, Rieger and another pastor, Steiniger, walked out of the second session in disgust at Heckel's refusal even to discuss a memorandum that the pastors had prepared listing their concerns. Heckel, for his part, had to return to Berlin with his tail between his legs. All he could take back was a statement he himself had drafted expressing his own views and which he claimed had had the unanimous support of the pastors in England (his legalistic rectitude at this point failing him since not all of them had even been present). Only Schreiner of Liverpool had found reassurance in Heckel's repeated declarations that all was really well in the German church. Heckel had also found some appreciation in a number of Bonhoeffer's Sydenham parishioners who attended a reception for him at the German embassy, but Bonhoeffer dealt with these in a meeting late into the night shortly after. Heckel also met with Bell at the Athenaeum but the reception there, as would be expected, was no more than polite. The London pastors issued their own statement refuting Heckel's claim to a unanimous welcome to his views and reiterating their opposition to any departure from the historic confessions of the Evangelical Church and to any imposition of the Aryan clause.

Nor was that all. Heckel on his arrival in London had first visited Bruno Schröder, perhaps in an attempt to drive a wedge between him and the pastors (the pastors certainly suspected this, and told Heckel so). The baron and his wife entertained Heckel hospitably, and Heckel may indeed have thought he had found an ally in the banker. Not so. Schröder afterwards was fully supportive of his pastors, and his letter of 19 February to Heckel is a model of courteous rejection. I am a man of patience, he says, needing time to consult with the congregations. Referring to a detailed report about dismissals and suspensions of pastors in that very day's *Times*, he asks Heckel: "to tell me frankly whether or not this is true, if it is, it would completely contradict what you said in your declaration, of which you so kindly left me a copy." And more in similar vein. It must have been some mild compensation, at least, to Heckel that shortly after this abortive London visit he was made a bishop and appointed head of the new Church Foreign Office. One of his first acts was to summon Bonhoeffer peremptorily to Berlin early in March and demand an assurance from him to disengage from further ecumenical activity. Bonhoeffer dutifully flew to Berlin but despite Heckel's browbeating categorically refused to give any such assurance.

What must have been even more disappointing to Heckel was that the gates of Lambeth Palace remained closed to him during his visit, as they had to Hossenfelder four months earlier. No invitation came from Archbishop Cosmo Gordon Lang. To make matters even worse, later in February an invitation *did* come from the archbishop – to Dietrich Bonhoeffer! Cosmo Gordon Lang was hardly the most dynamic or inspirational Primate of all England in modern times. He had spent his twenty best and most creative years as archbishop of York, and by the time he succeeded Randall Davidson at Canterbury in 1928 he was an ageing, tired and frequently sick man. One bishop said of his enthronement sermon that it "pleased everybody, and alarmed nobody." But Lang retained both a strong social conscience and a concern for Christian unity (in 1911 his had been a lone voice from the bishops' bench in support of Lloyd George's budget and he was one of the prime movers behind the "Appeal to All Christian People" issued by the Lambeth Conference of 1920). It was natural that he should be alarmed and concerned by what was happening in Germany. Interestingly, although Lang had been informed about Bonhoeffer by George Bell, the invitation to Bonhoeffer seems to have been conveyed not through Bell but H.W. Fox, general secretary of the World Alliance in England, which illustrates the importance of the different but related networks of contacts operating in England at this time. It followed a routine reception at Lambeth Palace on 19 February for foreign clergy working in London, at which Lang expressed his wish to meet Bonhoeffer. Word of this invitation in fact reached the Reich church office in Berlin before Bonhoeffer himself heard about it, to add to the discomfiture of all concerned. It was precisely the kind of engagement that Heckel and his office wished to block.

The interview with Lang took place at Lambeth Palace on 28 March and lasted 45 minutes. Bonhoeffer gave the archbishop as full an account as possible of recent developments. Lang was quite clear that there could be no recognition of the existing

Archbishop Cosmo Gordon Lang

Lambeth Palace: the gates remained closed to Hossenfelder and Heckel

church in Germany, and that he would never receive Heckel. He was, moreover, evidently appalled by what Bonhoeffer had to tell of him of his own recent treatment by Heckel in Berlin and the intimidating attempts to stop his ecumenical work. The archbishop was clearly impressed with his German visitor and hoped for another meeting soon. For Bonhoeffer himself it must have been of the greatest encouragement that the highest church figure in the land, and moreover leader of the worldwide Anglican Communion, had shown his solidarity with him and his cause. Not that he had any compunction about "disobeying" Heckel, whom he no longer recognized as having any authority and was therefore to be neither "obeyed" nor "disobeyed" but merely disregarded. This was a crucial stage in Bonhoeffer's personal combat in the Church Struggle – and it was fought out on English soil as much as in Berlin. Lang, for his part, in letters to the *Times*, in speeches and in interviews with the successive German ambassadors von Hoesch and Ribbentrop, was repeatedly to make clear his disgust at the treatment of Christians and Jews in Nazi Germany.

Meanwhile other people in London were taking an in interest in Bonhoeffer, and not just from church circles. *The Round Table* was a prestigious monthly journal on political and current affairs and its presiding editor was Philip Kerr, more gener-ally known by his aristocratic title Lord Lothian. Since 1925 he had been secretary of the Rhodes Trust, awarding scholarships to students from different countries to study at Oxford. He was to have a still more notable public career (cut short by untimely death in 1940) culminating as British ambassador to the United States 1939-40 – that crucial year when American material support for Britain's war with Nazi Germany was secured. At New Year 1934 George Bell was approached by Lothian in view of his intention to devote the March issue of *The Round Table* to the struggle for the soul of Protestantism in Germany. Bell gave a warm commendation of Bonhoeffer as just the person to write the kind of article that

Lord Lothian, Philip Kerr

was wanted, and it was agreed that Lothian, Bell and Bonhoeffer should meet. They did so over lunch on 16 January. Lothian was extremely interested in Bonhoeffer and all he had to say. But by then Bonhoeffer felt he must decline the invitation to write the piece. There had already been accusations in Berlin linking him with the reports on the Church Struggle in the *Times*, which he had truthfully and strenuously denied. But somehow word had reached Berlin that Bonhoeffer was assisting Bell with an article for *The Round Table*! Any overt authorship was now politically out of the question. But Bell did consult Bonhoeffer on the article he himself was about to prepare, which was to be an augmented version of an essay by the Swiss pastor and ecumenical worker Alphons Koechlin.

Bell was soon, partly in response to pleas from Bonhoeffer, turning his mind to another exercise for his pen. Through the early months of 1934 Bonhoeffer grew increasingly concerned for a clear word from the ecumenical organizations on where they stood with regard to the German church conflict. This was not simply an issue of principle (though it certainly was that) but a matter of practical urgency. Pastors who were being suspended or even imprisoned, and their parishioners, needed for their own immediate spiritual encouragement and morale an unmistakeable signal that the wider Christian world was in solidarity with them. The clearest form of such a message would be for the ecumenical world to sever completely all contacts with Muller's church as heretical and to deal only with the opposition. That was Bonhoeffer's aim, shared for a time at least by such as H.L. Henriod in Geneva. As chairman of the Universal Christian Council for Life and Work George Bell was the nearest thing to an official mouthpiece that the ecumenical movement as a whole had at that time. Bonhoeffer pleaded with him to make a definitive declaration. "The question at stake in the German Church," he wrote to Bell on 13 March 1934, "is no longer an internal issue but is the question of the existence of Christianity in Europe; therefore a definite attitude of the ecumenic movement has nothing to do with 'intervention' – but is just a demonstration to the whole world that Church and Christianity as such are at stake . . . Please do not be silent now! I beg to ask you once more to consider the possibility of an ecumenic delegation and ultimatum." A month later his pleading was even more desperate, as a result of a note from a beleaguered friend in Germany who had stated "in the present moment there depends everything, absolutely everything on the attitude of the Bishop of Chichester." August Jäger, a man with an already ruthless reputation as State Commissar in the Prussian Church, had just been appointed "legal administrator" by Ludwig Müller with the ominous charge to "complete the legal unity of the German Evangelical Church". Müller had

1.

32

Answer to the Peace-offer of the Reichsbishop of March 13th 1934

Reichsbishop has made an appeal for peace. God know's we would be only too glad if we could finish this hard struggle about our Evangelical church in a real and true peace. Truly we have not started this fight. In all our work and in the midst of this fight laid upon us we hope and pray and long for nothing more than for real healing power and for the true peace of our poor torn Evangelical church. According to our knowledge of the scripture and on the basis of our understanding of the confessions of the Reformation we cannot recognize the appeal for peace made by the Reichsbishop as the way towards real peace within our church. The solution intended by the Reichsbishop conceals the real fault, need and danger of the church. Therefore this solution cannot heal the disease of the church. On the contrary it threatens to aggravate this disease. Our main reasons are as follows:

1. there is in the message of peace made by the Reichsbishop a separation made between the confession and the exterior organisation of the church in a way which we cannot principally consent to. Christ is the Lord in heaven and on earth; he rules invisible and visible church. It is therefore that organisation, gouvernement and order of the church must be

further on it. The unity of exterior organisation which has been achieved on this way himself issued on 13 April a "Message on Peace in the Church" which announced that actions against church officers were to be called off. On the same day, however, a "Church Decree on the Pacification of the Situation in the Church" declared that Müller's amnesty did not apply to "actions with national political implications"! The Pastors' Emergency League almost instantly made a declaration in response to these decrees, stating emphatically that the real fault, need and danger of the church were being overlooked by Müller who was once again ignoring the whole question of the *confessional* basis of the church. Bonhoeffer soon had a copy of this declaration, and on 25 April made and sent a translation of it in his own hand to Bell.

Bell was thus being kept fully up to the mark with inside information from Bonhoeffer. Two days later, on 27 April, Bell and Bonhoeffer sat down together at the Athenaeum to discuss the idea of a pastoral letter to be sent to all churches involved in Life and Work, calling attention to the significance of what was happening in Germany. This letter would be issued on Ascension Day, 10 May. It was not, however, only Bell and Bonhoeffer who were involved in this venture. Joe Oldham had also been keenly following the German scene, had his own contacts in both Germany and Geneva, was in frequent contact with Bell and in fact sent Bell his own version of a draft for such a letter in mid-April. Oldham also was in more frequent touch than Bell with the American ecumenicals. On 2 May Bell sent copies of his proposed draft to Bonhoeffer, Oldham, Alphons Koechlin and Hans Schönfeld in Geneva. Bonhoeffer was greatly appreciative of the text but suggested several small yet significant changes. One especially deserves highlighting because it illustrates how at times even Bell did not quite grasp the sharpness of the theological issue as seen by the confessing opposition itself:

> You speak 'of the loyalty (of the pastors) to what they believe to be Christian truth'. Could you not say perhaps: to what *is* the Christian truth – or 'what we believe with them to be the Christian truth'? It sounds as if you want to take distance from their belief. I think even the Reichsbishop would be right in taking disciplinary measures against ministers, if they stand for something else but the truth of the Gospel (even if they believe it to be the truth) – the real issue is that they are under coercion on account of their loyalty to what *is* the true Gospel – namely their opposition against the *racial and political element as constituent for the Church* of Christ.

In fact it was to be a continual complaint by such as Bonhoeffer and Barth that the Anglo-Saxon world was congenitally prone to seeing the Church Struggle as primarily about "religious freedom" whereas in their view it was more than that: it was for the specific truth of Christ, not a general human principle however lofty: the *binding* of the conscience to the gospel rather than its inherent liberty. But it was a measure of the trust and respect in which each held the other that Bonhoeffer could write so frankly to Bell in this way and that Bell, equally, could accept the substance of Bonhoeffer's criticism. Bell's final text at the point at issue spoke of "the disciplinary measures which have been taken by the Church government against Ministers of the Gospel on account of their loyalty to the fundamental principles of Christian truth . . ."

Bell's pastoral letter in its final form was headed "A Message Regarding the German Evangelical Church to the Representatives of the Universal Christian Council for Life and Work from the Bishop of Chichester". It was put out on Ascension Day and two days later appeared in the *Times*. It is a short document, only about 540 words, but expresses amply enough the concerns felt by many regarding the imposition on the church of state-sponsored coercion and racial categories incompatible with Christian principle. It did not deliver the ultimatum Bonhoeffer had originally been hoping for, but he knew that Bell had gone as far as his official responsibility would allow. He was grateful and delighted: "In its consciousness it strikes at the chief points and leaves no escape for misinterpretation," he wrote to Bell. The ecumenical movement was beginning to find its voice.

Bell's effort, while modest even within his own terms, had come at a most critical point in the Church Struggle. On 22 April the Confessing opposition had met at Ulm and declared itself the one lawful Evangelical church in Germany before the whole of Christendom. Two weeks after Ascension Day, the free synod so long hoped for by the leaders of the opposition met at Barmen in the Ruhr and there, largely under Karl Barth's inspiration, drew up the famous Barmen Theological Declaration that clearly and unequivocally spelled out for the present context the true basis of Evangelical faith: "Jesus Christ, as he is attested to us in Holy Scripture, is the one Word of God which we have to hear, and which we have to trust and obey in life and in death. We reject the false doctrine that the Church could and should recognize as a source of its proclamation, beyond and besides this one truth of God, yet other events, powers, historic figures, and truths, as God's self-revelation." In six main theses this dichotomy between the affirmation of biblical faith and false teaching to be disowned was repeated in relation to the church's life, ministry and relation to the state. Thus was laid the foundation of the Confessing Church, and the Barmen Declaration still counts as one of the great affirmations of Christian belief and identity, as relevant as ever in a world where faith is prone to seduction by power, racism and nationalism. It still comes as a surprise to many people to learn that Bonhoeffer himself was not at Barmen, being preoccupied in London. But through what was said on Ascension Day he, Bell and Oldham had given a great gift to the Barmen synod: the awareness that the ecumenical world was with them, watching and waiting and praying. Nor do we find Bonhoeffer making much comment on Barmen at this stage. For him it was simply axiomatic that Barmen defined the true church and set its direction.

There was however another reason why we find relatively little mention of the Barmen synod in Bonhoeffer's letters during these days. His major preoccupation was with the ecumenical conference to take place on the Danish island of Fanø in August. Bonhoeffer while in London remained an active youth secretary of the World Alliance, maintaining contact with H.W. Fox, secretary of the Alliance in England, and G.H. Marten, archdeacon of Kingston-on-Thames, who was chairman of the English section. Sadly, Arthur Burroughs died in 1934. But Bonhoeffer's pastoral and other commitments were often too heavy to allow his attendance at all the relevant committee meetings. Nor was he able to attend a meeting of the World Alliance executive in conjunction with an important Life and Work conference in Paris in April on "The Church and the State of Today". The Fanø conference, 22-28 August, was in fact to be twofold: the biennial meeting of the Council of Life and Work in conjunction with the management committee of the World Alliance, and concurrently a youth conference sponsored jointly by Life and Work and the World Alliance. It was largely Bonhoeffer's responsibility, in cooperation with the secretaries H.L. Henriod and Theodore de Félice in Geneva, to organize this youth event. As well as all the usual questions about programme, travel arrangements, subsidies etc that organizing such conferences involves, there were especially fraught issues this time. Paramount was the question of who should actually attend from Germany. Barmen, Bonhoeffer believed, had made clear which was the true Evangelical Church of Germany. Reich church representatives should not be invited – and if they did attend, Confessing Church people would excuse themselves. As far as the youth conference was concerned Bonhoeffer got his way, though for a time he seriously considered withdrawing. The German youth participants were people whose credentials were either vetted by Bonhoeffer, or whom he already knew and trusted as his former students. The result was that no actual church representatives from Germany attended the youth conference, while at the Life and Work meeting both Confessing Church and Reich church representatives, including Heckel, were present.

The *Times* of 17 August 1934 under the heading "Church and State: Topics for Danish Conference" outlined the main themes to be dealt with at Fanø, highlighting the issue of conflict between church and state and "the European situation". "The speakers at various sessions of the conference are expected to include Lord Dickinson . . . the Bishop of Chichester, the Archdeacon of Kingston, Professor Stefan Zankow of Sofia, and Herr Bonhoeffer." It was clear that, coming so soon after Barmen, the Fanø conference as a whole would prove critical for the ecumenical movement. Would it, as Bonhoeffer hoped, follow the logic of Bell's Ascension Day letter and take a decisive stand with the Confessing Church? Theodor Heckel delivered a tediously unimpressive lecture. In a farcical incident worthy of a Gilbert and Sullivan opera he was joined late on by a German Christian spokesperson, Walter Birnbaum, who arrived in a privately chartered seaplane from Copenhagen having assumed that the conference would be taking place in the Danish capital, and then entertained the meeting with a speech of such trite ineptitude that even Heckel must have been embarrassed. Perhaps helped by all this, Fanø proved decisive. A resolution was passed condemning the autocratic church rule in Germany and expressing solidarity with those standing for the evangelical faith. It was a clear taking sides with the Confessing Church – though a tiny clause expressing the wish to remain "in friendly contact" with all Christian groups in Germany was to cause trouble later on. Much else happened at Fanø. The lines were set for the Oxford Conference of 1937 on "Church, Community and State" and Joe Oldham was appointed to be in charge of the preparatory study process. Moreover Dietrich Bonhoeffer and Karl Koch, president of the Confessing Synod, were both co-opted onto the council of Life and Work.

Bonhoeffer himself made two formal presentations. The first was his paper on "The Universal Church and the World of Nations" in which he (again!) called for a much stronger theological basis for the World Alliance. The paper is a critique of both the justification for war as being necessary for national self-preservation, and of secular pacifism based on ideals of human good and rationality. To both, Bonhoeffer opposes the divine command: You shall not kill. Intriguingly, among the English participants at this session was someone not normally associated, then or subsequently, with church-related deliberations: Richard Crossmann, then a fellow of New College, Oxford, a rising socialist and destined to be a minister in successive Labour governments in the post-war years. Crossmann had been pointed towards Fanø, and Bonhoeffer in particular, by George Bell. He was highly critical of Bonhoeffer's paper and the ensuing discussion, both of which he felt showed the naïveté of unconditional pacifism. But Bonhoeffer's theological premises are easily missed. Not organization but prayer and fasting will be the answer, he says. War is a symptom, not the root of the evil itself. "It is not pacifism that is the victory which overcomes the world . . . but faith, which expects everything from God and hopes in the coming of Christ and his kingdom. Only then will the cause of evil – that is to say, the Devil and the demons – be overcome."

Bonhoeffer's second formal contribution was his biblical meditation, given

Richard Crossman, 1936

at a devotional session, on Psalm 85:9 "I will hear what God the Lord will speak: for he will speak peace unto his people, and to his saints." Some sentences from this homily have become among the most widely quoted Bonhoeffer texts: "There is no way to peace along the way of safety. For peace must be dared. It is the great venture . . . Peace is the opposite of security." It also included his call for a universal ecumenical council of the churches to be convened and to declare against war: a call not heeded at the time (nor, it has to be said, evidently pursued by Bonhoeffer himself) but half a century later retrieved as one of the inspirations for the "Conciliar Process on Justice, Peace and the Integrity of Creation".

So much happened at Fanø and so much has been written about it, that it easily overshadows a follow-up event, almost insignificantly tiny by comparison as far as numbers go, in which Bonhoeffer was involved with two English participants from the youth conference: E.C. Blackman and Trevor Kilborn. The plan had been for a small consultation of British, German and French Fanø delegates to meet and discuss further issues on church and state resulting from Fanø. At the invitation of Jean Lasserre, Bonhoeffer's friend from his year in New York and who had also been at Fanø, the group met 4-8 September at Bruay in the Artois, northern France. From one point of view the meeting was a near-disaster since for not entirely clear reasons the French delegation (apart from Lasserre himself) never showed up, to Bonhoeffer's extreme annoyance. So it was left to three Germans (Bonhoeffer and two of his former students Jürgen Winterhager and Winfried Maechler), the two Englishmen and Mrs Kilborn attending as a guest, and Jean Lasserre. What they did was to launch into a discussion of the theme: "The ultimate authority for us Christians in proclaiming the Gospel." Small the group may have been, but it represented in microcosm and to fascinating effect the encounter between the Anglo-Saxon and Germanic thought-worlds. The English largely took the line expounded by J.H. Oldham in his preparatory paper for Fanø, that the essence of the gospel "was the *supremacy of the personal*: that the origin and authority are to be found in the life and mind of the Christian community which may or may not at any given time be the organized Christian Church". This approach drew no sharp distinction between Church and State "since the supremacy of the personal could be concerned in either". The Germanic emphasis, by contrast, drew the traditional sharp Lutheran distinction between the church as the body of Christ and the state as God's institution for preventing an evil world falling into chaos. Remarkably, however, the group as a whole determined to agree on a resolution to submit to the governing bodies of both Life and Work and the World Alliance. In summary, this statement affirmed the duty of the church, while not as such entering into political struggle, to study, through its members, social and political questions with a view to action from the perspective of the will of God for society. The aim should be the building up of a state which allows freedom for the Christian life (Matthew 5-8 etc). "Further there are many ways in which the Church, *within its own membership*, can and should reproduce the Christian life today: e.g. church unity, community living, settlement of disputes between church members without going to law, liberal education." The primary task of the church includes identifying and criticizing those attainments of human society not in accord with the biblical vision of God.

Small this group may have been and somewhat inchoate its discussion, but it was in fact trying to wrestle with questions apt to be overlooked on the broad stage of the Church Struggle and the generalized "witness for peace". Barmen and Fanø had spoken strongly and dramatically of "church" and "state" as corporate entities. That was necessary, but if left to itself carried the danger of a grandiose, abstract discussion. What does the Church actually have to say to the state not just about its own rights and life but about society as such? What about the concrete responsibilities of *individual Christians* as *church members* and as *citizens*? And could one really separate these realms from each other? These were the practical questions that men such as Joe Oldham would be directing towards the Oxford Conference and dealing with in much of his subsequent work. Equally, they were questions that would eventually demand attention from Bonhoeffer himself in his wartime *Ethics* and his prison writings. There is a delicate but real thread to be detected running

The Bruay conference September 1934
(left to right: *J. Lasserre, J. Winterhager, D. Bonhoeffer, W. Maechler, E. Blackman, T. Kilborn*)

from this Bruay meeting to Bonhoeffer's effort in *Ethics* to overcome "thinking in two spheres". And the English had an important hand in weaving it.

For the moment there was enough to do in consolidating and building upon the achievements of Barmen and Fanø, both in Germany and elsewhere. There had been enormous interest created outside Germany by Barmen, and many of those who had been at Fanø tried to do their own follow-up work in their home contexts. One very evident sign of this came in London in October when Bonhoeffer received from J.H. Rushbrooke, President of the National Council of the Evangelical Free Churches (and general secretary of the Baptist World Alliance) a copy of a resolution passed by the council's executive committee supporting the resolutions on the German church situation passed at Fanø "and, impressed with the vital evangelical issues concerned, assures its brethren in Germany who are standing for the preservation of the liberties of Christ's Church and Gospel, of the sympathy and the prayers of the Evangelical Free Churches of this country." Such gestures were significant not least because the main

J.H. Rushbrooke

counterparts of the English free churches in Germany, the Baptists and Methodists, were proving far too complaisant with the Nazi order to satisfy the British nonconformist conscience, which was soon to see its values embodied in the imprisoned Martin Niemöller rather than anyone in the German free churches. The Baptist World Alliance had in fact held its congress in Berlin in August that year, amid some controversy in Britain and the United States as to the rightness of doing so under the swastika. Rushbrooke, who had close personal relations with and deep inside knowledge of Germany, had a tough job both then and right up to the outbreak of war in 1939 in persuading his fellow-Baptists not to be too dismissive of their quietist German brothers and sisters. Karl Koch, president of the Confessing Synod, responded with warm appreciation for the Free Church Council's statement.

As far as the Church Struggle went, one really major task was left for Bonhoeffer during his remaining time in London: to ensure that the German congregations in England clearly identified themselves with the Confessing Church and disowned the Reich church. In late October 1934 a second Confessing Synod met in Dahlem, Berlin, and resolved on a new church organization separate from the Reich church. Flesh was now being put on Barmen. In London Bonhoeffer swung into action. On 5 November 44 representatives of nine of the congregations in England met at Christchurch, London, and solemnly resolved that *"they consider themselves as belonging intrinsically to the Confessing Church* and that they will take up with the authorities of the Reich church and the Confessing Church the necessary negotiations arising from this." Of course storms ensued with Heckel and the Reich church authorities during the following weeks, and the front in England was not quite as united as at first seemed – Schreiner of Liverpool in particular having doubts. But early in the New Year 1935 Bonhoeffer's own two congregations endorsed the Association's resolution. After Bonhoeffer returned to Germany some of the initial enthusiasm waned. It may not have been completely lasting success, but it was most certainly a victory that brought credit to the congregations themselves and greatly encouraged the Confessing witness in Germany. In no other country in the world did the German diaspora make such a move. And it should be remembered that most of the people whom Bonhoeffer inspired to take this step were not pastors but the lay members of the congregations, at whose head stood the firm, aristocratic figure of Baron Bruno Schröder.

Binding up the victims

While still in Berlin in 1933 Dietrich Bonhoeffer had written – and even had published – a paper on "The Church and the Jewish Question". It was notable for being written during the first phases of the Third Reich's state-sanctioned hostility to the Jews, varying from dismissals of "non-Aryans" from government and civil service posts to the boycott of Jewish shops and businesses supervised by the brown-shirted storm-troopers. Bonhoeffer identified three possible tasks for the church in the current context. First, questioning the state on the legitimacy of its actions. Second, "an unconditional obligation towards the victims of any ordering of society, even if they do not belong to the Christian community." Third, "not just to bind up the victims beneath the wheel, but to halt the wheel itself." The third of these options is rightly seen as Bonhoeffer's radical move beyond any position then envisaged by the German Protestant community, and a prophetic foreshadowing of where his own commitment would ultimately lead – to political resistance. It should not however be read as diminishing in significance the second option, of binding up the victims, on which as Bonhoeffer says the church has an "unconditional obligation". This unconditional obligation, no less than the Church Struggle itself, was one that Bonhoeffer felt laid upon him almost the moment he arrived in London in October 1933. Victims from under the wheel were already arriving as refugees in England. Many more were still in Germany, actually or potentially in concentration

camps. Further, some of the most precious limbs of the German churches' missionary work overseas were being crushed out of existence. This area of need and
suffering was to be a major part of Bonhoeffer's ministry in London, and in facing
the challenges he was brought into further contact with some of the most outstanding British women and men then active on social and international issues.

In one sense Bonhoeffer had little choice. He did not have to seek clients to help;
they made a beeline for him. In January 1934, after just three months on London, he
writes to his brother Karl-Friedrich about the numerous people he has met, including "countless German visitors, most of them Jews, who know me from somewhere
and want something from me. I must have written already that a Dr Steiner was
here, whom you directed to me." As this letter implies many such people came to
him on the recommendation of a mutual acquaintance in Germany. Others came, as
always happens, because the pastor of an expatriate congregation of one's national-
ity is a natural port of call. Many came in great financial need for themselves and
their dependants. Others were hoping for openings and commendations to possible
employers. If Bonhoeffer had no choice about being sought for help, equally he
chose to help whenever he could even if his means were small and the suggestions
he could make were very limited. In all this a certain discretion had to be exercised.
Too high a profile being given to work among those who had fled the regime would
inevitably bring accusations of political hostility to the Reich, which while justified
would not make prospects for longer term work any easier.

Bonhoeffer's attitude to the refugee and asylum seeker is perhaps best described
as a way of life, a natural expression of that most ancient yet endlessly relevant
Christian practice of *hospitality*. The manse on Manor Mount was itself an open
house of refuge from the moment Franz Hildebrandt, under threat from the Aryan-
izing "German Christians", stepped through the door in November 1933. Other
friends and former students were to arrive, if not under the same kind of danger
then at least wanting respite from the increasingly insufferable atmosphere of
intimidation and mindless nationalism at home. Jürgen Winterhager and Wolf-
Dieter Zimmermann were among these. Zimmermann recalls affectionately the
seemingly chaotic regime in the house: the huge, late breakfasts, the discussions
and arguments that often went on till the small hours of the morning, the joyous
interventions of music-making, not to mention the sheer horseplay at times. It all
seemed far distant from the cafés on the Kurfürstendamm where you had to keep
your voice down. Another visitor to Sydenham was Herbert Jehle, a physicist who
was keenly interested in theology and ethics and withal a convinced pacifist. He had

joined Bonhoeffer's student circle in Berlin and moreover attended the Fanø conference in August 1934. During 1933-34 he had a research studentship at Cambridge and was able to visit Bonhoeffer a number of times. (One of his visits caused a scene fit for the stage of farce. He arrived at Manor Mount one evening, and finding Bonhoeffer still out decided he would give him a surprise on his return and lay down under the Bechstein piano. Bonhoeffer did arrive much later and went to bed, to be woken an hour or so afterwards by a strange, sonorous noise downstairs. Investigation revealed a sleeping Jehle snoring his head off. The incident concluded with wild hilarity all round.) Bonhoeffer's parents and other family members also appeared during these months.

Bonhoeffer used his contacts to try and assist individuals whenever he could. In July 1934 for example he wrote to Reinhold Niebuhr in New York, enquiring whether there existed in the USA an organization to which émigré students (Jews or those expelled for political reasons) could turn for help in furthering their studies or re-training. In London, he says, a committee has been formed to help such academics but has almost no money. "Here in London I am especially concerned about a 23-year-old man who used to be chairman of the Republican Student League, a law student, who really is in need and for whom I cannot find a place. I don't think he is especially brilliant, but he simply must be helped. I'd like to know whether there is a possibility in the States for him to carry on with his studies or to begin new ones, perhaps a scholarship or whatever. That is one case. Another is that of the author Armin T. Wegner – Tillich will certainly know him – very left-wing; he has had a terrible time in a concentration camp, a complete breakdown. He has not been able to find anything here and is in despair."

In late July 1934 a visitor with a special claim on Bonhoeffer's attention arrived: Hans Wedell, a lawyer from Düsseldorf and husband of Dietrich's cousin Gertrud (née Bonhoeffer). Wedell, though a "non-Aryan", was not at the moment himself a refugee (though a few years later was compelled to leave Germany) and was serving as legal adviser to the Confessing Church in the Rhineland. His main concern was to solicit help for "non-Aryan" Christian youth in Germany, and he was anxious

Hans and Gertrud Wedell

to meet George Bell. Bonhoeffer immediately wrote to Bell on his behalf, stressing not the claim of kith and kin but rather his character as "a very definitely Christian man and very active in his congregation . . . He is a very serious and conscientious man." Wedell was able to continue his work but was suspended from his church post in 1935, whereupon he embarked on theological study, first in Germany and then in the USA, and became a pastor. He and his family emigrated to England just before the outbreak of war in 1939 and Hans himself spent the war years in the United States where he entered the Congregational ministry. After the war, reunited, he and Gertrud were to run the ecumenical conference centre at Oakenrough. The first connections that such people made in the early 1930s with key English figures like George Bell often only came to their fullest significance years later.

Circumstances dictated that some enquiries could not be dealt with so positively. At New Year 1934 Bonhoeffer received a letter from Heinrich Lebrecht, a pastor in the Church of Hesse. Lebrecht was both non-Aryan and an outspoken voice in the Confessing movement, and was by now under serious threat from the dominant "German Christians" in Hesse. He wanted to know from Bonhoeffer what possibilities there might be for a pastorate in one of the German congregations in England. Bonhoeffer had to point out frankly that not only were all the pastorates occupied at the moment but it was very unlikely that as a non-Aryan he would be given permission to come by the Reich church office. But Bonhoeffer concluded significantly: "However, at the point where you as a non-Aryan are obliged to leave your post as pastor, I believe that in the English church here many doors will be opened to you. I urge you to let me know *immediately* when that happens. I am sure I will be able to help." Bonhoeffer's cautionary advice about not relying upon the official Reich church channels proved amply justified; Theodor Heckel in fact wrote to Lebrecht's bishop saying that as a non-Aryan Lebrecht should be discouraged from seeking a ministry within "German colonies" abroad where someone from his background would prove a divisive influence! Equally, however, Bonhoeffer's promise in effect came good, when in 1938 Lebrecht received from George Bell an invitation to come to England with his family.

But such cases as Bonhoeffer could deal with personally were just a few drops in a swelling stream of need and suffering arriving in England. Just before Christmas 1934 Bonhoeffer met with Joe Oldham over dinner and poured out his heart on the matter: he estimated there were about 3,000 in England, mainly middle-class professionals – lawyers, doctors, artists, journalists and the like. Next day Oldham wrote to one of his contacts about Bonhoeffer's "heavy burden of anxiety" about the refugees. "About half are Jews and are fairly well looked after by the Jewish community. The other half are in a bad way, and Bonhoeffer is in touch with several cases of actual destitution. Their anxiety is increased in some instances by not knowing whether their permit will be renewed after every six months. Is there any kind of action you can think of that might be taken to help these unfortunate people?"

The person to whom Oldham was communicating Bonhoeffer's concern was Eleonora Iredale, an Anglican member of the Council of Life and Work and one of Oldham's most important collaborators on the practical level for more than a decade to come. Known even to her friends as a "difficult" person (she seemed to be able to quarrel with just about anyone) she nevertheless had one indisputable and unsurpassable asset in the kind of situation now being addressed: an ability for finding and raising funds, and it was this that ensured her place on many an otherwise unwelcoming committee and working group.

Eleonora Iredale

Bonhoeffer also turned to George Bell, especially as in January 1935 with the Saar plebiscite in view a further wave of refugees seemed likely. Bonhoeffer reckoned that 30-35,000 could be expected if the vote went for incorporation into the Reich. "I am thinking of taking a few children and giving them into the homes of my people in the congregation. But how is the whole problem going to be solved, not individually but fundamentally?" Bell queried Bonhoeffer's high estimate of the size of the predicted exodus – correctly as it turned out since no more than 8,000 eventually fled the Saarland. But the overall numbers of refugees were large enough, and growing. Bonhoeffer and Julius Rieger visited Bruno Schröder in the autumn of 1934, and he gave generously to both pastors. Towards the end of January 1935 however Bonhoeffer had to appeal to Schröder again: "Now these funds have long since been exhausted, and in the meantime members of my congregations have given me a great deal of help. As of today, frankly, as a result of these needs my personal bank account is completely empty. That I could manage, except that I know there are two people expecting money from me tomorrow, who otherwise will have nothing to eat, and in three days there will again be others. What should I do? I have told these people that this cannot go on, and they understand, but they can find no other source despite all their efforts, and they are Protestant Christians with nowhere else to turn for help." Schröder was anxious to help but preferred to give through a recognized charity so that his contributions would be exempted from income tax. He suggested several organizations associated with the German communities in Britain but Bonhoeffer was doubtful about them, either because they were not actually sufficiently engaged with refugees, or were too "German Reich" in orientation. Bonhoeffer began enquiries as to whether his Sydenham church might itself set up a charitable fund, but as so often happens in the end it was the Quakers who came to the rescue: there came to light the Refugee Committee for Professional Workers, and Bonhoeffer pointed Schröder to its director, Mary Ormerod at Friends' House in Euston Road. Finally Bonhoeffer was able to write to Schröder overjoyed and grateful for his generosity. No less grateful was he that just before his departure back to Germany in April 1935, his two congregations at his request made special collections specifically for the refugees just as they had done for victims of one of the mining disasters in Britain and of an earthquake in Japan, and for the Bethel institution in Germany.

The plight of many of the refugees was pitiable enough. But what of those who not only could not get out of Germany but were in prison or concentration camp? International concern about conditions in the camps was already growing. A leader of this concern in Britain was Dorothy Buxton, one of the most outstanding women of her generation, already possessing an extraordinary record of activism for social justice and peacemaking. Dorothy Buxton (née Jebb) had, at the turn of the century, studied moral sciences and economics at Newnham College, Cambridge (though of course like all such female students at that time and for many years later she was not allowed to take a degree). She married Charles Roden Buxton, a Liberal MP who later, as did Dorothy

Dorothy Buxton

herself, turned socialist. Her concern for peace led her progressively towards Quaker belief and practice. During the 1914-18 war she founded the "Fight the Famine" council and with her equally gifted sister Eglantyne Jebb set up and for a time was secretary of the organization that was soon to become known by the name by which it is still world-famous, Save the Children. She left this to head a project providing press reportage from Germany in order to counterbalance one-sided reporting and propaganda. The Buxtons had a long and unusually close knowledge of Germany, and from the time of the Nazi advent to power Dorothy was campaigning to bring home to influential opinion in Britain the real nature of the regime and its brutality. In January 1935 she contacted Joe Oldham in view of her wish to make a visit to Germany soon, particularly in order to assess the attitudes of church leaders – especially on the concentration camps. Oldham immediately put her in touch with Bonhoeffer. As well as knowing most of the church leaders, Oldham advised, "He would be sympathetic on the subject of the concentration camps." But he issued a cautionary note on expecting too much public protest even by the Confessing Church just at the moment. Evidently well briefed by Bonhoeffer, Buxton was able to visit Germany. On her return, she reported that on the whole it was the Roman Catholic leaders who were more aware and concerned about the issues – the notable exception being Karl Koch of Westphalia, president of the Confessing Church Synod. Right up to the outbreak of war Dorothy Buxton continued to speak and write passionately about Nazi Germany and the need for wholehearted support of the Confessing Church.

There was one more category of victim at this time. Relatively unnoticed in many accounts of the Church Struggle is the fate of the German missionary societies such as the Gossner Mission, the Leipzig Mission and the Basel Mission (only partly Swiss). These organizations, often the offspring of particular regional churches and under their guardianship, had since early in the 19th century been among the jewels in the crown of German Protestantism in Africa, Asia and the Pacific. With the advent of Hitler's Reich and the corresponding desire by Ludwig Müller to centralize all church activities and incorporate them into structures under the German Christian label, the missions with their regional independence and theological diversity were especially vulnerable to the Nazi policy of *Gleichshaltung* ("coordination" or "conformity"). There were heated battles about a proposed new coordinating structure for the missions, with their leaders stoutly resisting demands by the German Christians for control. Such debates however during 1934-35 seemed increasingly academic because it seemed unlikely that any of the missions were going to survive under the Nazi economic order. The draconian measure forbidding practically all transfer of Reichsmarks overseas was having a devastating effect on the missions. Missionary staff were going unpaid and essential work was grinding to a halt.

It was now to Joe Oldham, saviour of the German missions from British depredations and hostility during and after 1914-18, that the leaders of the German missions turned in desperation. Oldham travelled to Germany in September 1934 to meet with their leading representative Siegfrid Knak. On his return Oldham reported on the danger of an imminent and total collapse of all German missionary work and went into overdrive in arousing the concern of church leaders both in Britain and the USA. In November Knak and a delegation from Germany came to London for further discussions, and a plan was drawn up by Oldham and his assistant at the International Missionary Council, William (Bill) Paton. This involved an emergency fund being raised, paid for partly out of contributions by British missionary societies and partly by voluntary gifts and donations from the church constituency at large. Remittances would be sent directly from this fund to German missions in the field. These remittances however would be regarded by the Germans only as loans, and within Germany the societies would pay into a German bank an equivalent amount until conditions allowed repayment to Britain. At best such a scheme could only minimize inevitable hardship, but it was a very practical gesture of solidarity.

Oldham in turn approached Bonhoeffer on the issue and it is clear that they discussed the matter in great depth. It is likely also that Knak and his colleagues spoke with Bonhoeffer while in London. Bonhoeffer immediately turned his hopeful sights on the City office of Bruno Schröder and shared his hopes that a sum of £50,000 might be raised. The baron would not make any ready promises but was more than willing to receive Oldham and Bonhoeffer together for an interview. In the end it was Oldham who saw Schröder on his own and by all accounts the meeting was successful. This was but one more example of how during these months in London the networking and contacts were so important and how, at different points and to meet a variety of needs, the currents of communication and appeal could run first one way and then another, around the Bonhoeffer-Bell-Oldham triangle – with Baron Bruno Schröder an essential power-source. A week in Oldham's diary in 1935 shows well the industry involved in such efforts among all his other commitments.

SUNDAY 20
2nd after Epiphany

MONDAY 21

TUESDAY 22

WEDNESDAY 23

THURSDAY 24

FRIDAY 25
Conversion of S. Paul

SATURDAY 26

Memo.

A week in J.H. Oldham's 1935 diary: note entries for Bonhoeffer, Knak and Schönfeld

Pastor and People

By now the obvious question arises: did Bonhoeffer have any time and energy left for actually being pastor to his two congregations? The answer is an emphatic yes. Bonhoeffer did not use his Forest Hill manse simply as a base for his activities on the grand stage of the Church Struggle and humanitarian work among refugees. His priority from start to finish was the ministry of preaching and pastoral care. "I have always wanted to be a pastor," he had written to Karl Barth. At New Year 1934 he had to apologize even to George Bell for not accepting another invitation to Chichester – " . . . there is just in the present moment so very much work in the congregation that I can hardly leave this place in this week." To his grandmother Julie Bonhoeffer he confesses himself continually amazed at how much is going on even in such a small community and how much work is generated for the pastor. Anyone who doubted their pastor's commitment would be brought up short by his remarks in the annual report of the Sydenham church for 1934:

> It makes little material difference whether the attendance at a worship service is large or small. The so-called 'success' of a pastor is really concerned least of all with the number of worshippers. But I would like to ask: does the average attendance of 40 during the last few months really correspond to the 140 names listed in the directory, representing some 280 persons who might be coming? Does a Sunday School attendance of six children, a confirmation class consisting of two children from one family, and a total of 42 contributing members, when the minimum contribution is as low as ten shillings and sixpence [53p in today's decimalised currency], truly correspond to the situation in this congregation? Or are there some inhibitions and obstacles, which with good will could be cleared out of the way?

It is salutary to reflect that throughout his life Dietrich Bonhoeffer rarely addressed congregations of more than 40-50 people. In the case of his time in London this did not in the least inhibit the seriousness of his preaching, though he admitted he found, for the first time in his life, having to preach *every* Sunday – at Sydenham in the morning and often at St Paul's in the evening – rather a strain. His sermons were handwritten or typed out in full. Twenty-three manuscripts (comprising just fragments in two cases), have survived, most of these having been sent by Bonhoeffer to his fiancée Elisabeth Zinn. Five are originally in English. Unfortunately we have none of his Easter sermons, nor any of what would been his early expositions of the Sermon on the Mount – although there are three based on verses from the Gospels of Matthew and Luke that clearly foreshadow the treatment of the call to follow Jesus to be seen in the early chapters of *Discipleship*.

By and large the sermons follow the church year: Reformation Sunday, Remembrance Sunday (the German *Totensonntag*, not the British commemoration of war-dead), Advent, New Year . . . and so on. But Bonhoeffer also kept himself free to present whatever he felt were the most urgent challenges of the hour. In the autumn of 1934 he preached a series of four consecutive sermons working through 1 Corinthians 13 – St Paul's "hymn of love" – deliberately designed to culminate on Reformation Sunday with the text "So faith, hope, love abide; but the greatest of these is *love*." The whole series was an attempt to place the Lutheran emphasis on "justification by faith alone" in its proper perspective and to rescue it from being acquiescence in lazy piety or abstract intellectualism. *"What does it mean to believe in Christ, who was himself love, if I still hate? What does it mean to confess Christ as my Lord in faith, if I do not do his will? Such a faith is not faith but hypocrisy. It does nobody any good to protest that he or she is a believer in Christ, without first going and being reconciled with his or her brother or sister – even if this means someone who is an unbeliever, of another race, marginalized or outcast. And the church that calls a nation to belief in Christ must itself be, in the midst of that nation, the burning fire of love, the nucleus of reconciliation, the source of the fire in which all hate is smothered and proud, hateful people are transformed into loving people. Our churches of the Reformation have done many mighty deeds, but it seems to me that they have not yet succeeded in this greatest deed, and it is more neces-sary today than ever."* Here too is a clear pointer to the coming themes of costly discipleship and community in Christ. This sermon apparently made an unusually deep impression on the congregation.

Bonhoeffer the preacher made few concessions to his hearers. Not that he used abstruse theological language – his speech is for the most part plain, even terse, and certainly rarely given to verbal decoration. But he was so *serious*, so *demand-ing* – not so much of intellectual effort but of decision and commitment. So many of the sermons are high-voltage eschatological announcements: God is coming! The restlessly holy and unbelievably loving God is invading this world in judgment and grace, offering not anodyne comfort and "assurance" but *eternal life*; not asking for a little bit more bourgeois piety and virtue but *demanding heart, soul, life and everything*. This is what some members, at Sydenham at any rate, found too discom-forting and evidently why the congregation grew no larger. But if his sermons were never tritely embroidered, at times they were dramatically illustrated with stories from the everyday and public world. For Advent Sunday 1933 he chose the text Luke 21:28: "Now when these things begin to take place, look up and raise your heads, because your redemption is drawing near." The previous Sunday there had occurred at Grassmoor, near Chesterfield in Derbyshire, a mine disaster that took a number of lives, and the national newspapers were full of this latest tragedy underground (relatively frequent occurrences in those times). Bonhoeffer begins his sermon with a vivid account of how horrific it must be to utterly trapped and alone in the darkness deep underground, helpless to do anything but wait . . . for the sounds of rescue coming nearer. *"And he listens, beside himself with concentration, as each*

News Chronicle: *the mine disaster at Grassmoor, Derbyshire gave Bonhoeffer his cue for his Advent Sunday sermon, 1933 (© The Daily Mail, used by permission)*

blow comes nearer. Each passing second seems like an hour, he can't see anything at all, but he can hear the voices of his helpers, then at last wild, desperate hammer blows ring in his ear. Rescue is at hand, only one more step and he will be free. You know don't you, why I am talking about this on Advent Sunday? What we have been talking about here is Advent itself. This is the way it is. God coming near to humankind, the coming of salvation, the coming of Christ . . . stand up and raise your heads, because your redemption is drawing near." Then follows an exposition of what such coming rescue might mean, for the imprisoned, the sick, the oppressed and humiliated in every way.

Surprisingly, perhaps, there are few direct references to events in Germany and the Church Struggle, though we have earlier noted Bonhoeffer's highly personal sermon on Jeremiah of January 1934 in which he cannot forbear to mention the

The Daily Telegraph: *Hitler's bloody purge of the 'Röhm Putsch' sent new shock waves all over Europe*
(© The Daily Telegraph, *used by permission*)

people captive by faith to Christ in Germany. But it takes little effort or imagination to detect the background or the allusions to be drawn, the relation between text and context. Nowhere is this more so than in his sermon for 8 July 1934, on Luke 13:1-5, the reaction of Jesus to the massacre of Galileans by Pilate, concluding with ". . . but unless you repent, you will all likewise perish". Five days earlier there had occurred the so-called "Röhm Putsch" and Hitler's massacre of suspected Nazi dissidents. Over 100 reportedly died in the bloodbath that sent new shock-waves around Europe, the latest confirmation of the brutality of the regime (Bonhoeffer himself heard from his brother-in-law Hans von Dohnanyi that 207 was the actual figure). Bonhoeffer called on the congregation first of all not to run away from such ugly events on the public scene and seek some pious refuge away from it all. "Perhaps this text frightens you, and you think it sounds too much like the news of the day – too dangerous for a worship service." Just as there are people who do not like to attend a funeral because it brings them too close to death, so there are devout people who try to hide from the dark side of life. And then there are the *moralistic* people who subtly try to distance themselves from ugly events by asking first "Who is to blame for this?" By contrast, Jesus calls on *us* all to *repent*, to seek God and fullness of life anew.

Any reader of these sermons today, seventy years on, has of course to ask, "Am I hearing the same sermon as the first hearers did in St George's or St Paul's?" The words are the same. But the preacher is now, inevitably, different for us from the Pastor Bonhoeffer who delivered them then. It is virtually impossible for us to read them without the perspective of his later life and eventual fate bringing the words into a certain relief. Therewith also lies the danger of reading into them extraneous or anachronistic meanings. Bearing that in mind, nonetheless, the reader who assumes that certain ideas only belong to Bonhoeffer's later thought can be surprised at several points. Not only are we on the way to *Discipleship*, but also to some of his prison writings. Or, it would be better to say that in his prison writings he was sometimes retrieving elements that had long been part of his thinking. Very striking, for example, is his sermon for Trinity Sunday 1934, based on 1 Corinthians 2:7-10 and comprising an exposition of the true meaning of "mystery" in human thought and experience. He says at one point:

> . . . *mystery does not mean simply not knowing something.* The greatest mystery is not the most distant star; to the contrary, the closer something is to us, the better we know it, the more mysterious it becomes to us. The person farthest away from us is not the most mysterious, but rather the one next door And the mystery of that person will not be diminished for us, the more we find out about him or her: instead, he or she will become ever more mysterious to us, the closer we come together.

Ten years later in prison in his "radical" writings he would be speaking in similar vein: "The transcendental is not infinite and unattainable tasks, but the neighbour who is within reach in any given situation." "The beyond is not what is infinitely remote, but what is nearest at hand." Then there is his remarkable sermon, preached in English at St Paul's in 1934, on 2 Corinthians 12:9: "My strength is made perfect in weakness." It is an attack on the Nietzschean dismissal of Christianity as a "slave-religion", an offence to the strong and powerful. The weak (here Bonhoeffer was thinking particularly of the handicapped in such institutions as Bethel in Germany) are neither to be despised nor patronized with benevolence from above. Christianity sees weakness as made holy by God, who himself became weak in Christ. God's own self is seen in suffering. Christianity means a devaluation of all human values, and a new order of values in the sight of Christ. *"Not the weak has to serve the strong, but the strong has to serve the weak, and this not by benevolence but by care and reverence . . . Why is suffering holy? Because God has suffered in the world from man, and wherever he comes, he has to suffer from man again. God has suffered on the cross. It is therefore that all human suffering and weakness is sharing God's own suffering and weakness in the world. We are suffering: God is suffering much more. Our God is a suffering God . . ."* Here one could almost be reading the letters from prison of 27 June, 16 July, 18 July, and 21 July 1944 . . . "Only a suffering God can help." Finally, it is impossible to overlook what Bonhoeffer has to say about eternal life in the light of his last known words before execution in April 1945: "This is the end, for me the beginning of life." "That life only really begins when it ends here on earth, that all that is here is only the prologue before the curtain goes up – that is for young and old alike to think about," he dares to say on Remembrance Sunday 1933.

There is the old joke about the member of a congregation being asked by a pious relative whether the minister of his church was a godly man, and receiving the answer: "Well, he has two of the divine attributes – invisible on weekdays and incomprehensible on Sundays." Bonhoeffer was certainly not incomprehensible in the pulpit – indeed perhaps too comprehensible for some of his hearers. Neither was he invisible during the week, in the homes of the people and on the church premises, or on the tennis-court with Laurence Whitburn and others. He sang with the choir at St Paul's – they performed not only that diehard favourite of English evangelicalism, G.H. Maunder's *Olivet to Calvary* at Passiontide but also the Brahms *German Requiem*. He *tried* to improve the singing at Sydenham with limited success. He quickly introduced the new German hymnbook for overseas congregations. But at Sydenham both people and organist were prone to progressive deceleration of tempo during the course of a hymn. One Sunday Bonhoeffer and Lawrence Whitburn conspired to deal with this by singing at full volume the correct speed from verse to verse, the only result being that halfway through the first hymn they were a full verse in front of both organist and congregation. At last a small choir was established that eventually graduated to singing some carols under the Christmas tree. (Bonhoeffer's views on the role of music in church are well expounded in his sermon for Cantate Sunday 1934 based on Psalm 98:1.)

Nor was Bonhoeffer too busy to have contact with other local clergy and their flocks. He made a point of attending the Monday morning meeting of ministers in Forest Hill and one of them, Ernest Reeve, quickly invited him to preach to his own Sunday evening congregation at Perry Rise Baptist Church. One of Bonhoeffer's hearers that night was Fred Collins, then a young teenager, who still recalls how impressed everyone was that this German visitor could deliver such an evangelical message – and in such excellent English.

Another pulpit from which Bonhoeffer surprised a congregation: Perry Rise Baptist Church

He shared in the lives of his families, the birthday parties and the picnics. To some he became especially close. At Sydenham he conducted the confirmation class for Ingrid Elisabeth Cruesemann and her brother Gerhard Eduard, the confirmation service itself being held on Palm Sunday 1934. The photograph of the two young people and pastor – who on this picture looks scarcely older than them – taken at the church door is one of the most charming from this period of Bonhoeffer's life. He later also confirmed the son of Philip Cromwell, a lawyer. There were baptisms, funerals and at least one wedding. In showing pastoral care he could be impulsively generous; distance, time and money being no object. When Lawrence Whitburn and his wife moved away from Sydenham to the northern outskirts of London, Bonhoeffer still frequently came to see them. On one of their cinema visits Julius Rieger found

his friend deserting him in the midst of a film, whispering that he had remembered an urgent pastoral case he must attend to. And when Rieger's wife Johanna gave birth to their second child, Bonhoeffer, undaunted by a journey involving two changes of trams, arrived with an enormous bouquet of cornflowers and marguerites, having bought up the entire stock of these blooms in the florist's shop in Forest Hill.

Perhaps no incident better illustrates where Bonhoeffer felt his priorities lay than the illness and death of 19 year old Gertrud Lütgens

Bonhoeffer and his confirmands Ingrid Elisabeth and Gerhard Eduard Cruesemann, Palm Sunday 1934

in April 1934. This young woman from Hamburg had been in London only since October the previous year. She fell ill with appendicitis and died on 7 April. Bonhoeffer had still been considering whether to travel to Paris to attend the important study meeting of Life and Work on "Church and State", but it was this tragedy which finally made him decide against it. He conducted the funeral and burial service on 11 April. Gertrud Lütgens' starkly simple, lonely headstone still stands in Bromley Hill Cemetery, bearing the single legend '*Auf wiedersehen*'.

'Auf wiedersehen' – the grave of Gertrud Lütgens

The happy couple, Frank Goetz and Doris Dickens

A month later, at the St Paul's Church, a contrastingly happy celebration took place: the wedding of two long-standing members of the congregation, Frank Goetz (a master butcher) and Doris Dickens. They had met and fallen in love through their membership of the church choir. Bonhoeffer for his sermon text took Ruth 1:16: "For whither thou goest, I will go; and where thou lodgest, I will lodge: thy people shall be my people and thy God my God . . ." The homily is a simple, unadorned but moving meditation on love, human and divine, and the dependence of the former on the latter. *"To be married in a true Christian sense means to be able to pray together. We thank God, that he has been with you all your life-time, that he has made you faithful members of his congregation. You were baptized, you were confirmed in this church, you have been taking part for many years in the most beautiful activity*

The wedding reception: Pastor Bonhoeffer stands with the bridal party (St Paul's church, Aldgate)

of our Church, in the church-choir, it is true to you that you may say to one another today: Thy God is my God. You will take all your love, all your faithfulness, from Him who alone makes life worth living and love worth loving." The pastor afterwards presented the couple with a signed Bible and a copy of the sermon, and joined the large number of guests at the wedding reception. Rita Colman, daughter of the Goetzes, tells of her paternal grandmother writing to her parents just after their marriage: "Pastor's sermon at the church was very nice and comforting, note 'My God shall be your God, my people shall be your people.' Also his encouraging speech at the dinner table." No less was she impressed by the fact that "then pastor danced with us two mothers". Indeed, Rita Colman repeatedly heard in her upbringing that Pastor Bonhoeffer "was such a lovely person".

Besides the dramas of joy and sadness, however, every parish and pastorate has its weight of humdrum routine and niggling detail to bear. Any who imagine that Bonhoeffer's career, even in London, was so adventurous as to be spared "the trivial round, the common task" should take a quick look at the minutes of his church council meetings. The need to find flower-arrangers for the altar, or someone to pump the organ, arrangements for Christmas nativity plays . . . and of course the accounts presented by the treasurer . . . not even a Bonhoeffer could escape these.

India and non-violence

Even as he sailed to New York in 1930 Dietrich Bonhoeffer had been starting to dream of visiting the East and India in particular. At that stage the wish seems to have been born out of a general desire to encounter the exotic, the worlds of eastern mysticism and spirituality that would offer such a contrasting foil to his native western Protestantism. How would the worlds of the Buddha and the Upanishads appear to a Barthian? By the time of his London pastorate, however, the longing for India was fused with his newer passion: to explore non-violence and life in community as the concrete fulfilling of the Sermon on the Mount. It is a beautiful paradox that Bonhoeffer's fervent loyalty to Karl Barth's emphasis on Christ alone as the revelation of God should now drive him in turn to look beyond the "Christian West". So in a letter from London in May 1934 we find him telling his grandmother Julie Bonhoeffer: ". . . I'm thinking again of going to India. I've given a great deal of thought lately to the issues there, and believe that there could be important things to be learnt. In any case it sometimes seems to me that there's more Christianity in their 'paganism' than in the whole of our Reich church. Christianity did in fact come from the East originally, but it has become so westernized and so permeated by civilized thought that, as we can now see, it is almost lost to us." Likewise to his former fellow-student at Union Seminary, the Swiss Erwin Sutz, he almost explodes in his frustration at what he says is a virtual betrayal of Christ by western Christianity and his German background in particular:

> National Socialism has brought about the end of the church in Germany, and has pursued it single-mindedly. We can be grateful to them, in the way the Jews had to be grateful to Sennacherib . . . And while I'm working with the church opposition with all my might, it's perfectly clear to me that *this* opposition is only a temporary phase on the way to a wholly different opposition, and that very few of those involved in this preliminary skirmishing are going to be there for that second struggle.
>
> I believe that all of Christendom should be praying with us for the coming of resistance "to the point of shedding our blood" [Hebrews 12:4] and for the finding of people who can suffer it out. Simply suffering is what it will be about, not parries, blows or thrusts such as may still be allowed and possible in the preliminary battles; the real struggle which perhaps lies ahead must be one of simply suffering through in faith. . .

> You know, it's my belief – perhaps it will amaze you – that it is the *Sermon on the Mount* that has the deciding word on this whole affair.

Karl Barth had spoken of the "wholly otherness" of the biblical God. Bonhoeffer wished to find this "wholly otherness" earthed in following Jesus and the Sermon on the Mount. And he felt in turn that Indians such as Rabindranath Tagore and Mahatma Gandhi might be the ones from whom western Christians might have most to learn. He also shared his thoughts with Reinhold Niebuhr in New York. Niebuhr was somewhat sceptical about whether the kind of passive resistance being practised against British rule in India could make any difference against the Nazi tyranny in Germany.

It was not accidental that it was in London during 1933-35 that Bonhoeffer's interest in India, and Mahatma Gandhi in particular, grew so intense. For it was exactly at this time that the inter-war constitutional debate about the future of India, the jewel in the imperial crown, was at its height with the sessions taking place of the Round Table that would eventually lead to the India Act of 1935. In opposition to this Gandhi was at one of the peaks of his influence in India and of his reputation abroad. Among progressive opinion in Britain there was huge interest in Gandhi and much popular support, notwithstanding Winston Churchill's dismissal of him as the "half-naked fakir". Bonhoeffer avidly read Gandhi's autobiography *The Story of My Life* and referred to it in at least one of his London sermons, and devoured whatever else of and about Gandhi that he could lay his hands on. There was, moreover, one other figure important in communicating Gandhi's vision. *Madeline Slade* was the

Mira Behn with Mahatma Gandhi in London

daughter of a British admiral. She took India as her adopted country and Mira Behn as her Indian name. In due course she became a close associate of Gandhi, living his simple life-style and also at times being imprisoned herself, and becoming a powerful advocate of his views. She frequently visited Britain for this purpose and also accompanied Gandhi to the Round Table conference. Bonhoeffer went to hear her speak in London at least once during one of these visits.

Woodbrooke

None of this, of course, would compare with actually visiting India, meeting with Rabindranath Tagore and staying with Gandhi in his ashram. For this he needed introductions. Here C.F. Andrews (see page 18) was important, and he encouraged Bonhoeffer to visit Woodbrooke, the Quaker house at Selly Oak, Birmingham where he would meet a number of people closely involved, like Andrews himself, with India and pacifism. But the actual letter of commendation to Gandhi on behalf of Bonhoeffer was written by George Bell. Gandhi in November 1934 in turn wrote cordially to Bonhoeffer assuring him that he and his companion (it is not clear whether this would have been Julius Rieger or Herbert Jehle) would be welcome to stay with him if he was out of prison, otherwise in one of his institutions, and gave details of costs and living conditions.

Circumstances were finally to prevent the passage to India. But Bonhoeffer's interest in communities of peace and non-violence suffered no diminution and India was not the only inspiration here. Only relatively recently has it emerged that while in London, through one person in particular, Bonhoeffer encountered another movement that excited him in this pursuit, namely the *Brüderhof community*. This had been founded at Rhoen in Germany in the 1920s by Eberhard Arnold, a Protestant strongly influenced by evangelical revivalism but – more in line with the historic Anabaptist or Mennonite traditions than with later pietism – driven towards a discipleship based on communal living and pacifism as concrete obedience to the Sermon on the Mount. Not surprisingly the Brüderhof community did not sit comfortably with the new Nazi regime in Germany, especially as the authorities wished to take over its school for children. The school was therefore transferred to Liechtenstein and the community as such in due course removed itself to the United States. In the meantime Eberhard Arnold's son Hardy came to England in the summer of 1934 to take a course in education at Birmingham University – where of course he would also be close to Woodbrooke at Selly Oak. According to Hardy Arnold himself it was through Martin Niemöller that Bonhoeffer came to hear of the Brüderhof. Quite how and when the actual contact between Bonhoeffer and Hardy Arnold was made is not clear, but they met at least twice in London (once, at Bonhoeffer's urgent request, in a tea-shop) and possibly at Selly Oak too. Evidently Herbert Jehle shared in at least one of these meetings. There was a clear mutual interest, and Hardy Arnold excitedly reported on the conversations in letters to his father. There were also certain clear differences of approach. The Brüderhof was a community of men and women and families, while Bonhoeffer was mainly interested in celibate communities of men preparing to be pastors. The Brüderhof saw itself as a new kind of church completely separate from the state, while Bonhoeffer envisaged a quasi-monastic community serving the wider church that still (as the Confessing Church) claimed to be the true Evangelical Church of Germany. The Brüderhof emphasized the "leading of the Spirit" whereas for Bonhoeffer there had to be a more decidedly Christ-centred direction and control of the community. But both Hardy Arnold and Bonhoeffer felt that essentially they were allies in a common endeavour to rediscover community in Christ the peacemaker as the reality of the church. Once again, Britain had provided Bonhoeffer with an opportunity for encounter, dialogue and learning – and this with a fellow-German – and one that would have been far from easy in Germany itself at that time.

As a final footnote on how Bonhoeffer's reflections on non-violence were encouraged in Britain, in February 1934 he received in the post from Eric Gray Hancock, an acquaintance of Bonhoeffer's student Jürgen Winterhager, a copy of *Cry Havoc* by Beverly Nichols, an account of the experiences of a pacifist during the first world war.

The theological colleges and religious houses

Sometime in the 1960s John Wright, a Methodist minister in England, was sorting through old papers and items accumulated over the years, prior to moving house. He came across a journal he had kept while a theological student at Richmond College, on the western edge of London, in the 1930s. Idly curious at rediscovering his youthful past he began turning the pages, and found that his jottings prompted recall of incidents long since erased from memory. But nothing prepared him for the shock of reading in his own handwriting the entry for 4 October 1934: "*Tonight we had a visit from Dietrich Bonhoeffer of the University of Berlin, one of the leading young Barthian theologians and one of the most important figures in the German Church situation. He gave us a splendid talk on Barth's theology and the situation in Germany. . .*" Then came back into his mind's eye the picture of a young German academic, pink-faced and fair-haired, quietly spoken and polite to a fault, whom he had escorted around the college on that visit.

Bonhoeffer's invitation to Richmond College had been facilitated by Rudolf Weckerling, a Berlin acquaintance who had been a German exchange student at Richmond. It was indeed an unusual privilege for English theological students to hear someone speaking straight out of the heart of the German Church Struggle. Not that all were evidently completely impressed. The neo-orthodoxy of Karl Barth and Emil Brunner had yet to make its fullest impact in Britain and some of the students, more attuned to the religious import of psychology and evolutionary science,

Richmond College staff and students 1934-35. John Wright who took and kept notes on Bonhoeffer's lecture is in the second row from front, seventh from the left.

Africa

West Africa.

ENT? COL.		DIED
1844	J. R. Wayte	1846
1862	M. Grimmer	1871
1872	J. W. Bell	1874
1872	W. Penrose	1877
1874	R? Lamb	1878
1871	Elijah Bew	1879
1883	A. R. Clegg	1886
1884	J. W. R. Stead	1887
1885	A. Bromwich	1887
1887	A. C. Matthews	1891
1883	Bryan Roe	1896
1891	W. F. Somerville	1896
1890	Henry J. Ellis	1899
1888	C. R. Johnson	1899
1895	E. Brownscombe	1901
1897	Fred? A. Lees	1902
1903	Arthur G. Jubb	1906
1883	Alfred G. R. Bartrop	1910
1907	R. E. Newton	1928

South Africa.

ENT? COL.		DIED
1857	Edwin Millier	1866
1860	George Scott	1875
1868	Gardener Scates	1877
1877	Jos? Culshaw	1881
1879	Will? Greig	1886
1862	Rich? Hayes	1888
1884	Geo. S. Sheldon	1890
1843	John Wilson	1891
1878	R. Walton Lewis	1892
1880	George A. Theobald	1897
1874	G. A. Chalker	1899
1859	James Fish	1901
1894	W. Eacott	1907
1869	G. Weavind	1916
1901	R. M. Brown	1916
1877	S. R. Ravenscroft	1926
1886	John Howard	1926
1879	G. Spargo	1902
1877	R. Abraham	1924
1878	G. Golightly	1927
1909	Ebenezer O'Lartey	1927
1879	Samuel Clark	1928
1879	Harvey Wilkinson	1928
1860	S. Horner Stott	1929
1877	George Lowe	1930
1878	John W. Househam	1930
1875	Robert Matterson	1931
1877	J. Harvey Gathercole	1932

Egypt.

1878	G. W. Baxter	1884
1872	R. S. Eckersley	1891

The Africa missionary memorial board, Richmond College

reportedly listened with puzzlement to one who sounded to them almost like a fundamentalist. But John Wright wrote in his journal a clear outline of the main points of Bonhoeffer's lecture, which dealt with the competing claims to authority of logic, psychology and history – all of which are confronted with the only truly ultimate authority of the crucified Christ. Here Bonhoeffer certainly was no fundamentalist: "Be it an infallible church, Book or Doctrine, all these assume that there is a spot in the world which is not fallen and thus exempt from sinfulness. But the only part of the world free from sin and its positive correlative is Christ Jesus . . ." John Wright concluded his record: ". . . Many other questions came – on experience and conscience and a few on politics and on the purpose of preaching. Afterward I had a word with him and saw him off."

Whatever the impact made by him there, Richmond College and one of its features in particular made an unforgettable impression on Bonhoeffer. In the entrance hall there hung the memorial boards recording the names of former students who had died on the foreign mission fields. Bonhoeffer was almost overwhelmed by the list of those who during the late 19th century had died in Africa where disease had taken many so quickly that their dates of ordination and death were poignantly close together. Close by the boards a plaque bore the verse:

> They marked the footsteps that He trod,
> His zeal inspired their breast,
> And following their incarnate God
> Possess the promised rest.

The sight of the boards etched on Bonhoeffer's mind an indelible picture of costly ministry that he was often to share with his own students at Finkenwalde in the coming years. Richmond College was closed in 1972 and the building sold, but the memorial boards are still on view, and no less impressively, in Methodist Church House, Marylebone Road, London.

There is very strong evidence that at about this time Bonhoeffer also visited Spurgeon's (Baptist) College situated on South Norwood Hill where it still stands. In fact, South Norwood being so close to Forest Hill it is hard to imagine Bonhoeffer *not* going there given his interest in finding out more about the English theological institutions. Quite possibly the contact was made through Ernest Reeve, pastor of the Perry Rise Baptist Church. As its name implies, the college owed its origins largely to Charles Haddon Spurgeon, the "prince of preachers" in Victorian London. The college's emphasis on producing evangelical preachers remained strong, and

Bonhoeffer was struck by the pledge made by students before entering the seminary in which they affirmed their intention to become a preacher and to conduct themselves accordingly. Indeed one of the features of English theological training, in all denominations, which most impressed Bonhoeffer was the close and active relation between the churches and their respective theological communities, in contrast to German Protestantism where theological preparation was largely in the hands of the university professors – a situation that Bonhoeffer now believed had contributed to the catastrophe in the church. Preparation for ministry had to involve life in community with spiritual discipline at the centre and not just an optional addition to academic work. Bonhoeffer was even daring to speak of Protestantism's need of a new kind of monasticism as the seed-bed of a ministry that could reverse the malaise of a compromised Christianity. Not that by "monasticism" Bonhoeffer envisaged a cloistered joylessness. He, and Julius Rieger too, could not help noticing a peculiar trait that marked English seminary life, namely, the seriousness with which *sport*, team-games especially, was taken.

Playing as well as praying together: a hearty struggle at Spurgeon's College

Walking the corridors at Richmond or at Spurgeon's he would have had to view not just memorial boards and the yearly group photographs of staff and students in rank order. Pride in athletic prowess (or aspiration at any rate) stared out from the photographs of soccer, cricket and tennis teams. He was to find the same phenomenon even in the high church Anglican houses, and it mightily appealed to him, though he would prefer that the sport should involve all and not just the community's finest. Community should involve playing as well as praying together. At Finkenwalde the seminarians were to be surprised at the expectation that as well as studying the Reformation confessions and homiletics they would all join in ball-games on the beach, whether orthodox soccer and rounders or robust inventions of their own.

Towards the end of 1934 this attention to theological learning within a community life began to take on an aspect more urgent than a merely personal interest. At the Dahlem Synod of October 1933 the Confessing Church resolved to set up its own structures separate from the Reich church, including seminaries for the training of pastors. Dietrich Bonhoeffer had already been approached with a view to being – at still only 28 years old – the director of one of them. It looked increasingly likely that the visit to India would have to be indefinitely postponed, and Bonhoeffer prepared to return to Germany by the end of the year. He decided to visit as many Anglican religious houses and theological colleges as time would allow and asked George Bell for introductions. Bell accordingly wrote to the heads of the Community of the Resurrection (Mirfield), the Society of St John the Evangelist (Cowley, Oxford), the Society of the Sacred Mission (Kelham), Cuddesdon (Oxford), Wycliffe Hall (Oxford) and St Augustine's (Canterbury), commending Bonhoeffer as an excellent theologian who "is very anxious to have some acquaintance with our methods in England, both with regard to training for the Ministry and with regard to Community life."

In fact Bonhoeffer did not return to Germany until the spring of 1935. He preached his last sermon in London on 10 March, and only then set off with Julius Rieger for his tour of the religious houses and seminaries. The itinerary was not exactly as originally envisaged. First they went to Oxford and the "Cowley Fathers" at the Society of St John the Evangelist. It is

Society of St John the Evangelist (Cowley Fathers), Oxford

not clear however whether they also visited Cuddesdon and the low-church Wycliffe Hall. From Oxford they continued to Birmingham and (for the second time?) the Woodbrooke Quaker centre in Selly Oak. (Bonhoeffer said he particularly liked the atmosphere there, including the opportunity to indulge his skill at table-tennis.) Kelham, close by Newark in Nottinghamshire where the Society of the Sacred Mission and its theological college were then situated, was the next stage following a brief detour to see Stratford-upon-Avon. Finally they reached Mirfield and the Community of the Resurrection, near Leeds in Yorkshire. Cowley, Kelham and Mirfield were all late 19th

Bonhoeffer serving

Society of the Sacred Mission, Kelham (aerial view)

century creations of the Anglo-Catholic tradition that sprang from the Oxford Movement.
But it was an eye-opener for the two Germans
how each community had its own profile and
personality. This, they were amused to note,
extended even to attitudes towards such matters
as smoking: at Cowley, they were told, smoking
was anathema and strictly forbidden; at Mirfield
it was permitted; in Kelham one *had* to smoke.

True to form, at Kelham they were received
by a bearded lay-brother whose pipe seemed
permanently alight. The founder of Kelham,
Father Herbert Kelly, was now of venerable age
but still a lively lecturer who himself chain-
smoked throughout his discourses, aided by
a pail of inflammable fluid standing by his
lectern, into which he dipped a wooden stick

Father Herbert Kelly

whenever a new cigarette had to be lit. Kelly was thought by some to be a kind of English forerunner of Karl Barth. Bonhoeffer and Rieger at any rate found his lectures captivating and were delighted to discover that some of them were on sale in mimeographed form. Years later, says Rieger, Bonhoeffer wrote asking to have sent on to him the copies he had mistakenly left behind in London. The visitors had lively evenings of talks and discussion with the students on the German Church Struggle. They also spent a memorable evening with A.G. Hebert, Kelham's prize Old Testament scholar, who received them in his monk's cell. There was much else to be impressed by at Kelham. As recently as 1928 the new Great Chapel had been completed, its huge central dome reckoned to be the second-largest concrete dome in England. Inside the chapel, the crowning glory was the life-size sculpture of Christ with St Mary and St John on the Rood, the work of the noted sculptor Sargent Jagger. Many saw in this work Jagger's preoccupation with suffering, born out of his experience in the 1914-18 war. (In 1973 the Mission left Kelham for a smaller house in Willen, and the buildings were sold to Newark District Council. The Rood figures now stand in the garden of Willen Priory.)

It was however Mirfield that provided Bonhoeffer with his deepest impression during the tour. The Community of the Resurrection, with its attendant college of the same name, had been founded in 1892 by Charles Gore, the most influential Anglo-Catholic of the later 19th century, and the community continued to reflect his high-churchmanship in matters both of liturgy and ritual and of social commitment at home and abroad. Bishop Trevor Huddleston, who prophetically roused the British Christian conscience on South Africa from the 1950s onwards, would become its most famous mid-20th century member. At the time of Bonhoeffer's visit Father Edward Talbot was the Superior, but perhaps the most venerable figure present was the aged

Father Edward Keble Talbot

Walter Howard Frere who had returned to live at Mirfield following his retirement as Bishop of Truro. Frere was noted as a liturgiologist: not in the dry technical sense but imbued with a passionate spirituality. As one of the high church figures present at the Edinburgh World Missionary Conference in 1910 he had created something of a sensation when during one of the periods of silent prayer he stood up in his monk's robes, flung wide his arms and implored ". . . regard not our sins but the faith of thy church and grant to her such peace and unity as may be in accordance with thy will!"

And in fact at Mirfield it was the life of corporate prayer that touched Bonhoeffer most deeply: above all the way in which through the cycle of the daily offices in the course of each 24 hours the community prayed through the whole of Psalm 119. The experience

Walter Howard Frere as Bishop of Truro

deepened Bonhoeffer's already strong attachment to the Psalter; and this, the longest psalm of all, increasingly held him captive with its reiterated plea of the one who wants nothing so much as to be allowed to live as a sojourner on the earth so as to be able to fulfill the beloved command of God. Years later, he was to encourage his students to work on the psalm both exegetically and meditatively.

Mirfield provided Bonhoeffer and Rieger with another educative experience of a rather different order. One evening they took themselves on a walk through the fields around the village, and came across a sheep lying prostrate, showing obvious signs of distress and seemingly close to death. They debated whether to try and find the farmer but as it was growing dark decided to make their way back to the community house in time for the evening office. They woke next morning with uneasy consciences about the poor animal and at the first free moment hurried back to the field where they had left it. They indeed found the sheep, now standing up and looking quite at ease – with her newborn lamb beside her.

Above left: *Mirfield, Community House of the Resurrection;* and above right: *Mirfield, Church of the Resurrection interior in the 1930s*

The visits to the colleges and monasteries were now complete, but Mirfield was not the northernmost limit of the tour as a whole. Bonhoeffer continued north for what was evidently his one and only visit to Scotland, to meet with John Baillie who had been among his teachers at Union Seminary, New York. Baillie had the previous year returned to his native land as professor of divinity at New College, Edinburgh. This may also have been the time when Bonhoeffer and Rieger inspected the Lake District together (see page 27).

So concluded Bonhoeffer's "London period". In mid-April he took grateful leave of Baron Schröder, George Bell and Joe Oldham. An "intermezzo" it may have been, but it was one without which the next movement of his engagement in struggle and resistance would hardly have been possible. He returned to Germany with his experience widened still further as pastor and ecumenical worker, thanks to the peculiar diversity of church life that Britain offered him and to which he was open, from the free churches and Quakers to high and low Anglicanism. Crucial contacts had been made and friendships cemented. New ideas and been allowed to germinate in the time, space and atmosphere given him on the offshore island of Europe.

CHAPTER 4

THE CONTINUING STRUGGLE
1935-39

Dietrich Bonhoeffer returned to Germany from England in April 1935 and quickly set about his new role as director of one of the Confessing Church's illegal, underground seminaries. The first task was to find a suitable location. After looking at possibilities in the Rhineland and the Ruhr the search moved eastwards, eventually lighting upon the Baltic coast near Stettin (in present-day Poland) and the village of Finkenwalde. Here, in a former school, built almost among the sand-dunes, Bonhoeffer's seminary was set up and the first batch of students arrived by mid-summer. Until it was closed by the Gestapo (two years later in the summer of 1937) this was to be Bonhoeffer's home and operational base. For the first (and only) time in his life, even more than in the case of his London pastorate, he was totally in charge of a project - with the chance of implementing his own vision and ideas. He lost no time in doing so. From the start the students were made to realize that communal living was the essence of their theological formation. As well as the lectures and seminars, there was the daily round of morning and evening prayer, and extensive periods of silent meditation. Even more startling was the introduction of the practice of confession. Each ordinand and staff member, including the director himself, was expected to choose another "brother" as his confidante. Soon rumours were abroad about the suspiciously "catholic" regime being imposed at Finkenwalde. Not all the students took kindly to it, but most came to see that the exceptional challenges of the time required exceptional spiritual stamina and discipline. Indeed, many of the Finkenwalde students were to find themselves either in prison or concentration camp at one time or another. Many were to perish during the war, the slaughterhouse of the eastern front providing the regime with one of the most convenient ways of disposing of pastors and others of doubtful loyalty. But among those who survived both Hitler and the war were some of the outstanding figures in the post-war period: people such as the theologian Gerhard Ebeling, and Albrecht Schönherr who from the early 1970s was the presiding bishop of the Protestant Church in the communist German Democratic Republic. Another survivor, without whom the Bonhoeffer story and our knowledge of it would be rather different, was Eberhard Bethge. Son of a country manse in Saxony, Bethge at first feared himself a little out of his depth among the other students, many of whom were sophisticated Berliners and Bonhoeffer's former university students. It was a surprise when the director asked Bethge to be his own confessor, but it marked the start of the most important male friendship of Bonhoeffer's later life.

Nor was Finkenwalde all work and prayer. There were vigorous ball-games on the beach, swimming in the sea, frequent spells of music-making, birthday parties and the like. What he had seen in the English theological colleges left its mark. Nor was any of this diminished when after some months a "House of Brethren" was set up alongside the seminary, a community of graduates who could both practise a deepened common life and serve as a kind of flying squad of pastors for congregations whose own pastors had been imprisoned. What Bonhoeffer had seen as the advantageous practices of Kelham and Mirfield, where "cloister" and college existed side by side, was being applied. There were continuing tangible reminders, too, of those visits to the English houses. In May 1936 there arrived at Finkenwalde a packet of books from Father Paul Bull

Father Paul Bull, Community of the Resurrection, Mirfield

at Mirfield, and as well as being deeply grateful, Bonhoeffer in turn asked him how he could get hold of a copy of *The Way of Holiness* by R.M. Benson, founder of the Cowley Fathers at Oxford. Significantly, Benson's book was an exposition of Psalm 119, the focus of so much of the impression made on Bonhoeffer at Mirfield. He was still trying to obtain a copy of it two years later.

The Finkenwalde years were in some ways the grimmest of the Church Struggle. There was a continual battering of Confessing pastors and students to conform and submit to "legalization" by the Reich church committees. Several of Bonhoeffer's own students opted for this way, to his sadness. Others had to face ostracism or imprisonment. Bonhoeffer and his loyal circle were dubbed "fanatics" by those who sought what they thought would be a sensible compromise. The leadership of the Confessing Church itself was often uncertain and was divided over issues such as an oath of allegiance to the Führer (required of pastors), and the total number of Confessing pastors was in sharp decline from the heady days of 1933-34. In 1937 Martin Niemöller began his eight-year imprisonment under special orders from Hitler. For Bonhoeffer himself it was therefore a time of near ceaseless stress and at times depression. Yet this was the context in which he produced the two gems that, after his prison writings, are his most widely-read works: *Discipleship* (first known in English as *The Cost of Discipleship*) and *Life Together*.

With so much concentrated effort now centred on remote Finkenwalde and on the inner struggles of the Confessing Church, it might have been expected that Bonhoeffer's contacts with Britain and elsewhere outside Germany would be almost completely severed. True, since the 1934 Fanø conference it had been virtually impossible for him to work any longer for the World Alliance, since it had been effectively shut down in Germany. But at Fanø he (and Confessing Synod President Karl Koch) had been co-opted onto the council of Life and Work and this was to be an important lifeline to George Bell, Joe Oldham and the like. What is more, the leaders of the Confessing Church knew that Bonhoeffer – almost unique among them in his fluency in English – was a most vital instrument for mediating with the ecumenical world. Not only so, but Bonhoeffer felt that the Confessing opposition could learn much from some aspects of the "English" style of church leadership. This, he felt, took seriously the notion of "policy" – in contrast to the Germanic tendency for the collapse of high-minded principle into brittle and divisive expediency whenever a new crisis arose. In fact, scarcely had Bonhoeffer returned to Germany in the spring of 1935 than he found himself with Joe Oldham again, at a meeting in Hanover of the Council of Brethren of the Confessing Church. This, together with Oldham's presence, had been summoned in view of the increasingly intimidating situation faced by the Confessing Church, with new waves of arrests of pastors and raids by the Gestapo on church offices. The meeting delivered a strong message via Oldham to George Bell and the staff of Life and Work in Geneva, that the ecumenical movement could not go on wavering between two opinions and, in line with the real spirit of Fanø, must recognize the Confessing Church as the true representative of Evangelical Christianity in Germany. Oldham reported this fully to Bell. But during the summer, Bonhoeffer himself was twice dispatched by Karl Koch to fly to England in order to keep Bell and others fully informed of the critical situation. For a few weeks Bonhoeffer must have wondered whether he had really left his London pastorate.

It is a long, complex and sometimes tedious story, but the nub of the issue between the Confessing Church and the ecumenical organizations was: who from Germany should they invite to their international meetings? This was a far from purely administrative matter. Life and Work was now, largely under Joe Oldham's skilful direction, organizing the major conference on "Church, Community and State" to take place in Oxford in 1937. But there was a reluctance, especially by the Geneva staff, to follow radically the decision taken at Fanø of identifying with the Confessing Church as the true representative of German Protestantism and to exclude the Reich church as represented by Bishop Heckel and others. The Confessing Church, and Bonhoeffer above all, felt that to compromise here would be to betray all that the Barmen Declaration had stood for, and all the risks and costly actions it had prompted in faithfulness to the gospel. There is no doubt that Bell and Oldham strongly sympathized with the Confessing Church at this point, while in Geneva Hans Schönfeld and H.L. Henriod wavered – as if Fanø's decision also to "maintain friendly contact with all groups in Germany" now outweighed the prime resolve to support the Confessing Church. (In fairness, it must be acknowledged that Bonhoeffer had not made relations with Geneva any easier by his tendency, during his youth work for the World Alliance, to pursue enthusiastically his own programmes without always keeping the Geneva staff fully informed. Geneva was – and remains today! – anxious about "duplication" of ecumenical efforts.) Bell and Oldham made known to each other their deep distrust of Heckel and his ability to manipulate the reasonable people in Geneva, but they were faced with a practical problem: if only Confessing representatives were invited to Oxford there was the strong possibility of their being refused travel visas by the German authorities. Better to ensure a Confessing presence at the cost of one or two Reich church people also being present – even Heckel. For their part, the Confessing leaders were also faced with a very real dilemma by their uncompromising stand: with their repeated absence at ecumenical meetings they risked cutting themselves off completely from the very movement and people whose solidarity they sought.

The outcome of these manoeuvrings was that no Confessing Church representatives were present at the meeting of the council of Life and Work in Chamby,

Switzerland in 1935. However, in August the following year, also at Chamby, Bonhoeffer, Karl Koch and two other Confessing Church representatives did attend the meeting, which made final preparations for the programme of the Oxford conference. The Confessing Church delegates kept their distance from Heckel and the Reich church group (it may not be accidental that Bonhoeffer does not even appear in the conference photograph, where Heckel occupies a prominent position on the front row). Bonhoeffer did not speak in the plenary sessions but worked intensively behind the scenes in informal discussion with Bell and others. He was especially grieved at the way in which a resolution prepared by Joe Oldham, Henry Leiper (USA) and Marc Boegner (France) on the Jewish question was scuppered by the other German representatives. As sometimes happens still today, interventions on "internal problems" were not welcomed by national representatives. Over the following months the arguments about German representation at Oxford dragged on. As late as February 1937 Bonhoeffer attended several meetings of the preparatory study groups in London. Eventually, however, the Confessing Church withdrew its intention to attend as it appeared that one German group under Reich church leadership would be required. But in any case the dispute became academic when the ministry for church affairs refused permission for *any* Germans to attend Oxford, with the exception of a tiny and ineffectual group from the free churches.

Bonhoeffer felt that in people such as George Bell and Joe Oldham he had trustworthy and sympathetic friends, fundamentally allied with the Confessing Church and doing their best to implement that solidarity and commitment within the constraints of rules and circumstances not of their own devising. So much for Life and Work. With Faith and Order it was quite another matter and this brings us to the most sore and unhappy point in all Bonhoeffer's relations with figures on the British scene. Faith and Order, the movement emanating from the Lausanne conference of 1927, promoted dialogue between the churches on questions of basic doctrine, ministry, sacraments and so forth as the means towards greater unity. It had a continuation committee, and its secretary was Leonard Hodgson (1889-1969). Hodgson was at that time a canon of Winchester Cathedral, with a reputation already established as one of the ablest theological minds in the Church of England. He had been both an Oxford don and a professor of Christian apologetics in the USA. Soon after arriving in Finkenwalde in the summer of 1935 Bonhoeffer received an invitation from Hodgson to attend the next meeting of the Faith and Order continuation committee in Hindsgaul, Denmark. On enquiring who else from Germany was invited, Hodgson replied that, among others, Bishop Heckel was expected. The committee,

Leonard Hodgson about 1940

Hodgson said, was "extremely anxious to have the advice of all branches of the Christian Church" in deciding on its programme for 1937. He went on: "I think you will understand our position when I say that we cannot, as a Movement, exclude the representatives of any Church which 'accepts our Lord Jesus Christ as God and Saviour.' Right from the start there has been a general invitation to all such churches, and we cannot arrogate to ourselves the right to discriminate between them."

Doubtless Hodgson thought that on behalf of the committee he was being fair-minded, generous even, towards the Confessing Church with the desire "to be guided in our deliberations by all sections of Christian thought" and the anxiety "that Germany should not be represented exclusively by the Reichskirche." But Bonhoeffer reacted to all this like a bull to a red rag. He replied with a lengthy and trenchant letter. What greater privilege could a theologian and pastor receive, said Bonhoeffer, than an invitation to a great ecumenical synod gathered to hear the word of our Lord Jesus Christ, of praying for the Holy Spirit to lead to the unity of all Christendom? Before Christ there could be no pharisaical self-righteous pretensions or accusations against others but only repentance and mutual, brotherly respect. But, he went on, the Confessing Church takes a fundamentally different position towards the Reich church as compared with its attitude towards all other churches in the world and wholly contradicts the claim of the Reich church to accept the Lord Jesus Christ as God and Saviour. The teaching as well as the action of the Reich church leaders clearly shows that it no longer serves Christ but the Antichrist: "Obedience to the only heavenly Lord Jesus Christ continues to be co-ordinated, nay, subordinated to obedience towards worldly masters and powers. The Reich Church thereby continues to betray the only Lord Jesus Christ . . ." In the light of Barmen, the Reich church government can no longer claim to compose the Church of Christ in Germany nor any part of it. The core paragraph of the whole letter reads:

No member of the Confessional Church . . . can thus recognize in the Reich Church a church which pays homage to our Lord Jesus Christ as God and Saviour; he must rather beseech God that He may confound the Reich Church Government as an instrument of the Antichrist. Being a minister of the Confessional Church I cannot attend an oecumenical conference unless it either excludes the Reich Church or ventures openly to charge both the Reich Church and the Confessional Church with responsibility. This, however, means actually to interfere in their conflict and effectively to pronounce a judgment based upon allegiance to the Word of God and duly established in the name of God's whole communion.

The fight being conducted in Germany, Bonhoeffer stated, was on behalf of Christianity everywhere – a call of ultimate warning to churches all over the world that may be attacked by the very same powers. If the ecumenical movement and Faith and Order in particular were to face up to this challenge and make a judgment, however painful and disruptive it might be, it could prove to be the regeneration of the whole ecumenical movement and all Christendom.

The bull had roared. Hodgson replied with an even longer letter seeking to explain patiently and reasonably that the constitution and rules of Faith and Order would not permit it to venture any such judgment as Bonhoeffer was asking for, and that moreover this would prove impracticable. It would require a full hearing of both sides, and an unduly prolonged meeting of the continuation committee. Furthermore, the Reich church leaders themselves would refute the claim that they denied Christ as God and Saviour. Faith and Order, unlike Life and Work, did not seek to commit the churches to joint action, but only to face each other in deliberation on an equal basis and without questioning each other's right to be at the table, facing differences honestly and "speaking the truth in love".

Bonhoeffer saw no point in replying further. Hodgson had a fair point as far as the aims and rules of Faith and Order were concerned. But Bonhoeffer was speaking from within a context where those very aims and rules seemed manifestly inadequate to the situation. Hodgson had a clear view of the nature of that part of the ecumenical movement in which he held responsibility. From Bonhoeffer's standpoint, the integrity of the ecumenical movement required that understanding to be questioned or at least widened. Hodgson saw his ecumenical organisation as a kind of seminar for theological discussion where everyone was equal before the moderator's chair. For Bonhoeffer there could be no equality where one party had forfeited its right to be called church – and moreover was enjoying privileges while the other party was being persecuted, harassed and imprisoned often with the actual connivance of the other side. Hodgson's position, it must be acknowledged, was quite different from that of the other leading Anglican in Faith and Order, A.C. Headlam (see page 40) who was unashamedly contemptuous of the Confessing Church. Hodgson was trying to be fair in what one might call a typically English and, dare one say, Anglican way. But fairness was not what the struggle in Germany was about.

Hodgson was to go on to a yet more distinguished career. In 1938 he would become Regius Professor of Moral and Pastoral Theology at Oxford (and in 1944 move on to the Regius Chair in Divinity). For two decades he would be one of Oxford's most gifted scholars and teachers, covering the areas of Christian doctrine, Anglican and ecumenical theology, ethics and apologetics. The culmination of his life's work can be seen in his 1955-57 Gifford Lectures *For Faith and Freedom*. He had a special gift for stating clearly what the real issues were in relating the Bible and traditional doctrine to modern thought. One student who himself went on to become a New Testament scholar of great repute was fond of quoting Hodgson's dictum that the real question to ask about the miraculous and "mythological" elements in the gospel stories was: "What was it about this person Jesus that led people to talk about him in this way?"

Bonhoeffer and Hodgson would have a face-to-face encounter in 1939. It led them no closer together, and in fact provoked some actual mutual antagonism. It must simply be accounted a sad failure of communication between these embodiments, respectively, of Lutheran confessional passion and Anglican reasonableness. It was not, after all, as though Hodgson was ignorant of what was going on in Germany and its significance. During 1933-35 he preached two university sermons in Oxford, published as *Democracy and Dictatorship in the Light of Christian Faith*. Their theological core is belief in God in Christ as one who seeks to win people by the free acceptance of his love. Near the end of the second sermon comes this finely-stated passage:

> We are tempted to abandon the hard and rocky part of educating democracies for free and willing co-operation in responsible self-government. It demands so great a sacrifice of our present comfort, its travail pains are the endurance of so much chaotic inefficiency in the conduct of affairs, that we are tempted to renounce God's method of *winning* men, and to substitute, under some such high-sounding name as the 'leadership-principle,' the method of putting

on shirts of brown or black or blue, and knocking them on the head. We are tempted to renounce God's aim to win *all* men into the brotherhood of His family, to revert to a narrow and selfish nationalism, seeking to exclude non-British or non-Aryan races from their equal rights with us as brothers and sisters in Christ.

All of which, one might well feel, expresses exactly what in the life of the church, in word and deed, the Confessing Church was standing for over against the Reich church!

Bonhoeffer's disappointment with Hodgson was not allowed to affect his relationships with his British colleagues as a whole. To Bell he could always confidently turn in commending actual or potential refugees from Germany in need of help. One such was Ernst Gordon, a "non-Aryan" pastor in the Confessing Church who was suffering growing harassment, being dubbed "the Jew-pastor" by local Nazis. Bonhoeffer wrote to Bell in 1935 on his behalf. Gordon left for Switzerland in 1937 and Bell was able to facilitate his eventual reception, with his wife Bettina, in England in 1939. Gordon was ordained an Anglican priest in 1940, and served as priest at Christchurch, Battersea, for 25 years, succeeded by a chaplaincy and teaching post at Greycoats Hospital, Westminster (a girl's school), and three years as Vicar of St Mary's, Great Chart, Kent. Throughout this long and fruitful ministry he maintained close contact with Germany and was deeply committed to work for post-war reconciliation until his death in 1991.

Ernst Gordon, 1940

Another English figure whom Bonhoeffer came to know and respect highly was (Sir) Walter Moberly, a close associate of Joe Oldham and an active member of the council of Life and Work. Bonhoeffer got to know him well at the Chamby meeting in 1936. Moberly had an unusual career straddling theology and public service. As a young man he had been a steward at the Edinburgh World Missionary Conference in 1910. While an Oxford philosophy don, he had written two essays in the controversial volume of liberal theology *Foundations* in 1912. He fought in the 1914-18 war and was decorated for gallantry. After a succession of senior academic

Sir Walter Moberly

posts in English universities, in 1935 he was appointed chairman of the University Grants Committee, the most powerful and politically influential position in higher education in Britain. He continued to collaborate with Oldham both in the Oxford 1937 conference and in Oldham's study groups and publications before, during and after the 1939-45 war.

Such contacts suddenly grew especially important at the more personal level for Bonhoeffer in 1938, the year of Munich and, in November, the fearful "Kristallnacht" of action against the Jews. Dietrich's twin-sister Sabine was married to Gerhard Leibholz who taught constitutional law at Göttingen University and was a "non-Aryan". The Bonhoeffers as a whole were a very close-knit family, but with the Leibholzes Dietrich felt a special emotional bond for two reasons. Firstly, Sabine, his twin had been his closest companion literally from birth. Secondly, Bonhoeffer had never forgiven himself for an unfortunate lapse when, on the death of Gerhard Leibholz's father (an unbaptized Jew) in April 1933 he had followed the advice of his superintendent who counselled against conducting the funeral of a Jew at that particular time. He soon regretted that decision and thereafter always felt under special obligation to stand by the Leibholz family. By 1938 their position in Göttingen was becoming intolerable. Leibholz's position as a university teacher was under severe threat. The children were suffering intimidation from their teachers at school. Hans von Dohnanyi's inside information from the government warned of imminent registrations, passport and travel restrictions on Jews. And the threat of war, with all that that might mean for the Jews inside Germany, was growing. Emigration could no longer be delayed and they decided on England.

On 9 September 1938, escorted nearly as far as Basel by Dietrich Bonhoeffer and Eberhard Bethge in another car, the Leibholzes with their two young daughters Marianne and Christianne made it across the Swiss border and a few days later were in London, met by Martin Böckheler, Bonhoeffer's successor as pastor at Sydenham. Bonhoeffer had naturally alerted him and the members of his two former congregations. He had also written to Bell (and to Walter Moberly) in view of Gerhard Leibholz' obvious hope to find an academic post. With his twin-sister and her family in England, it was now as if part of Dietrich himself were there. Their sojourn was

Sabine and Gerhard Leibholz at work in their London boarding house

to last eight years. For a time they had to endure the privations typical of refugees – unfamiliar language, financial hardship, travel restrictions, living in a succession of drab guesthouses and furnished lodgings – all overshadowed by a vain search for work by the husband and father. But the kindness and network of support provided by George Bell and others made life more bearable.

Meanwhile life was becoming ever more problematic personally for Dietrich Bonhoeffer himself. The Finkenwalde seminary had been closed by the Gestapo in July 1937. The work of training pastors continued, however, in a still more clandestine way. Students were assigned to "collective pastorates" in the remoter parts of Further Pomerania, working in parishes and being brought together at intervals in secret country houses. But a real problem for Bonhoeffer was looming as the likelihood of war drew nearer: the threat of conscription for his age-group. He believed he could not in all conscience serve in Hitler's army, but neither was he happy about implicating the whole Confessing Church in an act of conscientious objection that few in the church would support or even understand. By November 1938 he had to report any changes of address or longer holiday journeys – a first step towards conscription. He therefore started planning for a visit to England in early 1939, sanctioned by official duties for the Confessing Church that gave him leave of absence from his work in Further Pomerania, but with the intention of sorting out his own longer-term future. Once again, as in 1933, it was to be England that gave him the breathing-space.

England 1939

England 1939 was to be of special significance for Dietrich Bonhoeffer. His two visits were marked by a series of encounters running the whole spectrum of emotions: joy at reunion, pain at renewed strong disagreement, poignancy at parting, assurance in a new friendship, and continuing doubts and uncertainty about the future. They took place in scenes as varied as an Oxford college, a south coast seaside resort, a London garden and a main-line railway station.

Bonhoeffer, accompanied this time by Eberhard Bethge, arrived in London via Ostend on 11 March. Of course there was a joyful reunion with Sabine and Gerhard Leibholz and their girls. He was also delighted to be with Julius Rieger again, not to mention members of his former congregations to whom he preached at least once, and he spoke to a meeting in Bloomsbury of "non-Aryan" Christians. But as soon as possible he wrote to, and visited, George Bell at Chichester. Henrietta Bell's recollection of this visit is telling: "He came to lunch then

Dietrich Bonhoeffer with Eberhard Bethge (left) 1939

and I noticed a great change in him. He was much quieter, much more serious and evidently labouring under great personal strain. He wanted to stay in his own country . . . and he wasn't sure of his whole attitude to war. But at the same time there was a certain clearness and serenity about him." In private Bonhoeffer poured out his heart to Bell on the personal dilemma facing him: the only alternative to conscription or conscientious protest would be service somewhere outside Germany, perhaps on behalf both of the ecumenical movement and the Confessing Church. But would not this be flight rather than fight? It seems that Bell gently invited him to relax his scruples on this point and as a good counselor simply let him talk and talk, and listened. Certainly afterwards Bonhoeffer wrote gratefully to the bishop thanking him "for the great help you gave me in our talk at Chichester. I do not know what will be the outcome of it all, but it means much to me to realize that you see the great conscientious difficulties with which we are faced." A classic case of a good pastoral conversation!

Then, early in April, with Gerhard Leibholz and Julius Rieger he went to the south coast again, this time to Bexhill-on-Sea, where Reinhold Niebuhr was taking a holiday just prior to starting his first series of Gifford Lectures to be given at Edinburgh University on *The Nature and Destiny of Man.* The modesty of a place where nothing more exciting or strenuous seemed to be on offer than a genteel stroll along the promenade might have

Bexhill on Sea in the 1930s

Reinhold Niebuhr

seemed an incongruous setting for agonizing moral and personal decisions. But by the time Bonhoeffer returned to London it seemed that some of the difficulties had been blown away with the sea-breezes, thanks to Niebuhr's helpfulness. It was eight years since he and Bonhoeffer had been together at Union Seminary, New York, though they had corresponded at least once, and they had much news to catch up on and thoughts to share. Hearing from Bonhoeffer about his situation, however, Niebuhr immediately promised to get invitations for him to make a prolonged trip to the USA to visit his friends in the National Council of Churches and to lecture in one or more colleges. That at least would postpone the danger of military call-up and obviate the danger completely if war should come while he was away.

But another prime reason – indeed the official one – for coming to England had been to develop ecumenical contacts on behalf of the Confessing Church, which was finding itself in an increasingly isolated position vis-à-vis the ecumenical bodies. Highly important developments were afoot following the 1937 Life and Work (Oxford) and Faith and Order (Edinburgh) conferences. Plans had been agreed, largely designed by Joe Oldham, for a World Council of Churches (WCC). Its constitution had been agreed at a conference in Utrecht in May 1938, and a provisional committee appointed with William Temple, archbishop of York, as its chairman. In all these developments and bodies the Confessing Church was virtually unrepresented. Bonhoeffer on his London visit was mandated to try and correct this situation by contact with George Bell and others. The prime goal of the Confessing Church leadership was to secure a permanent representative to the ecumenical movement either in London or Geneva. Having given up on the Life and Work secretariat in Geneva, which in the person of Hans Schönfeld they felt was now effectively a tool of the Reich church, what about Faith and Order? Bonhoeffer therefore wrote to Leonard Hodgson, now professor at Oxford, requesting a meeting to discuss the possibility of a "permanent German secretary of the Confessional Church in Geneva or in London, and if not permanent then perhaps for a year or two." Hodgson agreed to see him, and Bonhoeffer travelled to Oxford on 29 March. Their meeting took place in Hodgson's rooms in Christ Church. It was long, involved and unproductive – and at times quite heated. This time Bonhoeffer, in contrast to four years earlier, was not asking for *exclusive*

Christ Church, Oxford

recognition of the Confessing Church over against the Reich church but merely for a recognition of its rightful existence as a church and for help in making its voice known. But once again Hodgson stuck by the rules of Faith and Order, as he made clear to Bonhoeffer in his résumé written next day. In the first place, he said, no church has direct representation on the continuation committee, which is appointed by the World Conference. The German Evangelical Church not having been present at Edinburgh, it was not in a position to have a representative on the continuation committee. That committee could *co-opt* representatives of those churches wishing to be represented on it. "For this purpose it is necessary to be able to have communication in each case with a central body having full confidence of the whole church, and be able to invite representatives in its name. We are advised that at the present time there is no such church, and that we must not attempt to treat the different groups as if they were separate churches." The most he would offer was for Confessing Church representatives to be invited as guests to the continuation committee or to work on the different commissions, for which some finance might be available. Bonhoeffer left Oxford with further disappointment and disillusionment. Precisely whose "advice" was Faith and Order taking, that the German scene should not be regarded as one where "separate" churches existed, when it was manifestly clear that the opposite was the case? All along the line such official ecumenical leadership, for all its claims to impartiality, was playing into the hands of the Reich church, due to its refusal even to consider the terms of the struggle as seen by the Confessing Christians. The question of whether the ecumenical movement can and should make a judgment about the "heretical" stance of a church would arise again with vigour in the 1970s and 1980s in relation to the Dutch Reformed Church and the apartheid regime in South Africa.

There was, however, a new star arising on the Geneva horizon and this brought hope to Bonhoeffer. As the first general secretary of the nascent WCC the provisional committee, largely at the determined instigation of Joe Oldham and William Temple, had appointed the Dutchman Willem Visser't Hooft. Now in his late thirties, Visser't Hooft had a sharp theological mind strongly influenced by Karl Barth, and within the ecumenical youth bodies had shown himself a brilliant organizer. Bonhoeffer had seen him at a distance at various ecumenical meetings, though they had never really met, and was keen to know him better. Visser't Hooft on his side had already used some of Bonhoeffer's ideas and writings in his preparatory work, alongside Joe Oldham, for the Oxford conference, so there was equal interest in meeting on his part too. While in London Bonhoeffer heard that Visser't Hooft was coming to England and

Platform 1, Paddington station

W.A. Visser't Hooft

would be seeing George Bell. He immediately wrote to Bell asking him for help in contacting and meeting Visser't Hooft. This proved – just – possible. The only time and venue they found mutually convenient was an hour or so on, of all places, Paddington station. They walked slowly up and down the long, open platform one (perhaps pausing by the station memorial to the railwaymen who died in uniform during 1914-18 with its poignant statue of a private soldier reading his letter from home?) and passing under the great clock that now seemed to be counting down the time to the start of the next war. Visser't Hooft was surprised that instead of beginning with the relations between the Confessing Church and the WCC Bonhoeffer launched into his personal dilemma about military service, as if the Dutchman had been his lifelong friend. He went on to talk openly about the coming war – ". . . Hitler would surely attack Poland in the summer or autumn and . . . this would lead to war on a large scale." Visser't Hooft sensed he had private information (this, we now know, was very likely through Hans von Dohnanyi) and found the whole conversation deeply moving. Coming just a few days after his fruitless meeting with Hodgson, Bonhoeffer for his part experienced new hope and encouragement in Visser't Hooft. They knew that in war communication between those within and those outside Germany, however risky, would be an ecumenical imperative. So, in a setting as mundane as can be imagined, there began and was instantly sealed a friendship springing from instinctive mutual trust and regard. It was to prove vital during the coming conflict, and Paddington station should therefore always be listed among the sacred sites of ecumenical pilgrimage.

Bonhoeffer extended his London visit to five weeks, partly because of the continual anxiety that war could break out sooner rather than later and partly simply to be as long as possible with Sabine and her family. He showed Eberhard Bethge and the Leibholzes round the sights of London. He went to see the film *Victoria the Great* made in 1937 to commemorate the centenary of that monarch's reign and starring Anna Neagle. So anglophile had he become that, Bethge tells us, "When he saw the ongoing history of this country that was now threatened, he confessed, he could not hold back tears of anger." He returned to Germany on 18 April.

At the beginning of June he was sailing to the USA, having taken up the invitations facilitated by Reinhold Niebuhr. Soon after arrival in New York he came to feel he had made a bad mistake. It *was* flight, after all. There followed momentous days of turmoil and indecision, finally resolved when he told Niebuhr that he had to return to Germany which was where he really belonged; that he would have no right to share in rebuilding Christian life in Germany after the war if he had not shared the sufferings of his people during it; that Christians in Germany would have to face the terrible alternative of willing the victory of their country which would mean the end of Christian civilization, or praying for its defeat so that Christian civilization might survive; that he knew which of these alternatives he must choose but could not do so in security. On 7 July he sailed east and homeward again. He did not go direct to Germany but via London where he stayed ten days with Sabine and her family, and was able to visit his cousin Gertrud Wedell and her family (see page 59) who were staying at St Leonard's-on-Sea. He also met with Franz Hildebrandt (now a refugee again) and with Julius Rieger, but was not able to see George Bell. He found that Reinhold Niebuhr had continued to be active on his behalf while in Scotland, since there arrived from John Baillie an invitation to deliver the Croall Lectures in Edinburgh the following winter. Bonhoeffer accepted (inconsequently, as it obviously proved, with the outbreak of war), proposing as his theme "Death in the Christian Message". So these days were not entirely a holiday, even with the family. One of the girls was being bullied by some children at school on account of her being German. Uncle Dietrich marched with her into the school and with his fluent English sorted matters out with her teacher. Then one day Rieger called while Dietrich was at the piano teaching the girls some English nursery rhymes, with the news that Paul Schneider, a pastor from the Rhineland, had been done to death in Buchenwald concentration camp, the Confessing Church's first martyr.

Their last meeting: Dietrich and Sabine in the garden of their London boarding house, July 1939

On 19 July the family waved Dietrich off from the station. Just before then, what is perhaps the most beautiful photograph in his whole life was taken, showing him and Sabine talking together in the garden of their London boarding house. It was their last meeting on earth.

CHAPTER 5

WAR AND RESISTANCE
1939-43

One of the most striking aspects of the second world war in Britain was that it was not only fought for democracy but that, to a remarkable degree, it was actually *carried out* democratically. Yes, there was censorship and a "ministry of information". Yet not only in parliament but in the press and on platforms up and down the country there was an extraordinary level of debate about both the conduct and the aims of the war. This was true above all of the churches, where a profound sense of crisis facing western civilization, of which the war was but a symptom, was registered. Almost as soon as the war started, for example, the first number of J.H. Oldham's weekly *Christian Newsletter* appeared with its lively mix of information and opinion, continuing till well after the war and read by thousands. Behind the scenes Oldham's study-group "The Moot", bringing together figures as diverse as John Baillie, Walter Moberly, the poet and critic T.S. Eliot and the sociologist Karl Mannheim, was at work. In 1942 the Christian Frontier Council emerged, another of Oldham's projects designed to bring together Christians and others with moral insights on secular problems. North of the border, chaired by John Baillie, the Church of Scotland's commission on "The Interpretation of God's Will in the Present Crisis" was engaging the church in a new encounter with public issues. George Bell's Penguin paperback *Christianity and World Order* had its first printing in 1940, focusing on the role of the state, peace aims, and the contribution of Christian unity to world peace. Later in the war he would make his famous speeches in the House of Lords against the area bombing of German cities. There were the "Religion and Life" weeks. There was the Peace Aims Group led by William Paton and involving prominent academics like A.D. Lindsay, master of Balliol College, Oxford and W. Zimmern. There was the short-lived but remarkable Roman Catholic initiative "Sword of the Spirit". There was the high-level Malvern Conference of church representatives in 1941. And, over it all, there was William Temple! His paperback *Christianity and Social Order* came out in 1942, the year of his migration from York to Canterbury, and made such a wide public impression that some have credited it with being the single most important factor in the post-war Labour election victory in 1945. Indeed the two years of Temple's primacy, cruelly cut short by his death in 1944, witnessed a welling up of Christian engagement with public issues unmatched in Britain before – or since – in its intensity and popular impact.

The contrast with the scene in wartime Nazi Germany hardly needs stating. The Gestapo and Joseph Goebbels' relentless propaganda machine reigned supreme. Any attempt to discuss "war aims" was treason, and even to be found listening in to the BBC overseas service was a criminal offence. Those who wished to consider any sort of alternative future, let alone plan resistance, had to do so in secret isolation. That in itself made those in the underground opposition hungry for any sort of contact with the outside world.

Dietrich Bonhoeffer was no exception here. Indeed it was precisely during the three and a half years of wartime before he was arrested in 1943 that we find him taking British life and thought more seriously than at any previous period of his life. Strange as it may seem, despite his own rich experiences in London and elsewhere, his diverse friendships with British people and his love of "the English" in general, hitherto he had engaged in relatively little actual dialogue with British theology or social thought – as compared, for example, with that in the USA. Involvement in political resistance and reflections on a new order for a post-war Europe were to change that.

Of course there was an immediate and profound personal reason why Bonhoeffer's thoughts should continually travel across the North Sea to England - his twin-sister Sabine and her family were now living there as refugees. The lot of the Leibholz family, especially in the early period of the war, was no easier than for most such "aliens" even though, in Sabine's words, "England relieved our souls". They moved for a time to St Leonard's-on-Sea. In the spring of 1940 Gerhard Leibholz was interned and taken to Liverpool. There were fears that he would join the many "enemy aliens" being transported to the dominions. Sabine and her children moved to Devon, and then to Oxford which seemed a more hopeful place to be since Gerhard was receiving a small scholarship from the World Council of Churches with the possibility of an attachment to Magdalen College (the Bell-Oldham-Moberly network had evidently proved its worth). Eventually Gerhard was released and joined the family in Oxford where they remained until after the war. He was able to do some teaching and involved himself actively in the ecumenical network of discussion and advocacy. He contributed, for example, to J.H. Oldham's *Christian Newsletter.*

Back in Germany, for the first months of the war, Dietrich Bonhoeffer quietly continued his work of training ordinands for the Confessing Church in the "collective pastorates" of Further Pomerania. It was in the summer of 1940 that he began to move into the realm of actual political resistance. His brother-in-law Hans von Dohnanyi was a high-ranking civil servant in the ministry of justice. A mole within the Nazi establishment, he had long been compiling a "chronicle of shame" detailing the atrocities being committed by the regime that were growing in enormity especially in occupied Poland and against the Jews in particular. He had from even before the war confided to Dietrich facts about the opposition to Hitler involving both civil servants and the military, and the abortive attempts at a *Putsch* that had already taken place. In fact much of the coordination between the civil and military wings of the resistance took place in Dohnanyi's office. On the military side the centre was in the *Abwehr*, the intelligence agency directed by Admiral Walter-Wilhelm Canaris. General Major Hans Oster was among other military figures involved in the leadership of the resistance. The ostensible function of the *Abwehr* was to gather intelligence about the political scene abroad and among Germany's enemies in particular. Under Canaris however it was secretly aiming to make contact with those abroad who might support an overthrow of Hitler. In the autumn of 1940 Hans von Dohnanyi had serious discussions with Bonhoeffer about the possibility of him being taken on by the *Abwehr* as one of its agents. The fact of his having many ecumenical contacts abroad would serve well as an official justification for his service – intelligence services had after all to use people of many different backgrounds and even dubious political credentials – but more to the point it would serve the even more clandestine task of communicating information about the resistance to circles abroad who would be vital to its success. Bonhoeffer agreed, despite all the moral risks involved in conspiracy – one that would eventually require an attempt at the assassination of Hitler. He felt an instinctive need to be in solidarity with those attempting to stop the horrors taking place in Germany's name. If guilt was to be incurred, then better the guilt accepted for the sake of others than the guilt of standing aside to protect one's innocence while thousands were being murdered. At the same time, being taken on as an official agent of the *Abwehr* would for a time at least exempt him from military call-up, the threat of which still loomed. So Bonhoeffer was taken on as an unpaid agent of the *Abwehr*, attached to its Munich office. In a carefully prepared memorandum for Dohnanyi, he listed the kinds of foreign contacts to whom he could provide access through his ecumenical credentials. They included British names that have featured significantly in this story: Lord Lothian (British ambassador in Washington but now in 1940 with only a few weeks to live), Richard Crossman and Walter Moberly.

Bonhoeffer remained in the service of the Confessing Church in the far east of Germany. He was given leave of absence for several periods to write his *Ethics*, which he envisaged as the culmination of his life's theological work. Some of this writing was done in the seclusion of the Benedictine monastery in Ettal, not far from Oberammergau in Bavaria and within easy reach of Munich. The *Ethics* deals with the big themes that had been haunting him increasingly: What does it actually mean to do God's will concretely in the world? What does responsibility before God and one's neighbour entail when there are no longer any adequate rules? What are the implications of God becoming human in Christ for the overcoming of that "thinking in two spheres" that had effectively gutted Lutheran capacity to act politically? And, most critically for those entering into the moral ambiguities of the conspiracy, does responsible action sometimes mean being prepared to become guilty for the sake of others? Bonhoeffer draws upon a wide range of thinkers in his own Germanic tradition – and beyond. He writes with an awareness of the wider context of "the west". In this broader sweep but there are some striking references to the British scene and its traditions. In the contemporary public world there are once more villains and saints. "Reality lays itself bare. Shakespeare's characters walk in our midst" and Shakespeare's histories show that "almost every crown is stained with guilt". Political action requires acknowledgments of the laws of "statecraft" but also the requirement for "pertinent action". Bonhoeffer expresses approval of the way in which in England "pertinent action is entrusted not the specialist but to the amateur" as a counterbalance to the necessary work of the specialist. There is an interesting brief comparison of W.E. Gladstone, the late 19th century Liberal Prime Minister, with his German contemporary, Chancellor Otto von Bismarck, as leaders embodying differing but valid understandings of the goal of historical action: "The greatness of British statesmen . . . for example of Gladstone, is that they acknowledge the law as the ultimate authority; and the greatness of German statesmen – I am thinking now of Bismarck – is that they come before God in free responsibility. In this neither can claim to be superior to the other . . . Neither can be the judge of the other. It is always for God to judge." On the more theological level he is implicitly critical of the traditional Anglican marriage between a natural theology and an incarnational theology as leading to "a peculiar natural-Christian grounding of the state" but at the same time he welcomes the questioning of this by "young Anglo-Catholics . . . corrected by a *theologia crucis* [theology of the cross]." Evidently Cowley, Kelham and Mirfield had left their mark. But here he very likely had in mind theologians such as V.A. Demant who had contributed an essay on Anglican understanding of the state in one of the preparatory study volumes for the Oxford conference. (Speaking of Anglo-Catholics, an encounter between T.S. Eliot and Bonhoeffer would have been fascinating. As far as one can tell it did not happen, though it so easily could have since Eliot was by the mid-1930s a close collaborator with both George Bell and Joe Oldham.)

It was a lonely life Bonhoeffer now led, banned from preaching and publishing, having to report regularly to the police on his movements and with continual enquiries from the Gestapo suspicious that his *Abwehr* involvement was simply a pretext for avoiding military service. His cherished companion was Eberhard Bethge who continued to assist in the work with ordinands. Together they made music whenever possible (Bonhoeffer on the piano or clavichord, Bethge on the flute or singing.) Often the members of the Bonhoeffer family circle involved in the conspiracy – his brother Klaus, Hans von Dohnanyi and others – would meet in the family home in the Marienburgerallee in Grunewald (the Bonhoeffer parents had moved there from Wangenheimstrasse in 1935) to play chamber music, which served also as a useful cover for conspiratorial discussion. They would listen to the BBC German broadcasts in the evenings, *pace* the Gestapo. And as Eberhard Bethge once told the writer, there was one particular overseas broadcast that Bonhoeffer always made sure he could tune into each Christmas Eve. Mention has earlier been made of his love of the English choral tradition, and the Festival of Nine Lessons and Carols from King's College, Cambridge, was an annual must for him. Evidently it was not just the music that cheered him, but the sense that here was a way of once again being connected to the universal Christian fellowship, the *una sancta* celebrating even in the midst of war the promise of peace; as the fourth lesson in the service says, of the earth being full of the knowledge of the Lord as the waters cover the sea.

There was however one further companionship now entering his life. His relationship with Elisabeth Zinn had not survived the demands of the Church Struggle in the Finkenwalde period during which Bonhoeffer himself counselled his students that now was not the time to think of marriage. Paradoxically it was during these even more perilous war years that he fell in love with Maria von Wedemeyer, almost half his age and whose confirmation class he had conducted. She was the granddaughter of Ruth von Kleist-Retzow, an aristocratic widow who

The choir of King's College, Cambridge, Christmas 1940

was a firm friend of the Finkenwalde seminary and who, after its closure, continued to entertain Bonhoeffer and his colleagues on her family estate at Klein-Krössin in Pomerania. The couple's engagement was not made public until after Bonhoeffer's arrest in 1943.

In October 1941 the first mass deportations of Jews from Berlin took place. Hans von Dohnanyi enlisted Bonhoeffer in an *Abwehr* operation code-named "Operation 7" that enabled a number of Jews, ostensibly recruited as *Abwehr* agents, to travel to Switzerland with the officially stated purpose of gaining intelligence about enemy thinking and planning. Bonhoeffer put at their disposal his ecumenical contacts in the neutral country to facilitate their reception. Of course they never returned, which naturally made the Gestapo suspicious. But most of Bonhoeffer's work within the *Abwehr* involved his own travels. In all he made six foreign trips during 1941-42: one to Norway with Helmut von Moltke, leader of the "Kreisau circle" of resisters; three to Switzerland; one to Sweden in 1942; and one to Italy.

His first visit to Switzerland was in February-March 1941, commissioned by von Dohnanyi and Colonel Oster of the *Abwehr* to explore what contacts through ecumenical channels the resistance might be able to make with allied governments, and also to lay preparations for "Operation 7". Almost the first thing he did once safely over the border was to pen letters to Sabine in Oxford and to George Bell in Chichester. He renewed contacts with his ecumenical friends in Basel and Zurich but his chief goal was Geneva, the office of the World Council of Churches and W.A. Visser't Hooft in particular. He gave graphic and detailed accounts of the growing horrors in Germany, of the situation of the imprisoned Martin Niemöller, and of the fact of real resistance to the regime. Visser t'Hooft was able to pass this information on to William Paton and George Bell in England. It filled many gaps in the obscure picture that the ecumenical world had of the current state of the Confessing Church and of the opposition. Equally Bonhoeffer was eager for news of that wider world. "It is touching," wrote Visser't Hooft to Bell afterwards, "to see how hungry people like him are for news about their brothers in other countries, and it is good to know that he can take back so much which will encourage his friends at home." That one hour meeting on Paddington station two years earlier had now borne fruit in an exchange of crucial significance and a relationship of unshakeable mutual trust and regard.

The second visit to Geneva, in September 1941, was for the same purpose. In a remarkable way it brought Bonhoeffer into as direct a dialogue with his British partners as could be imagined in the circumstances, through two books with which he was presented on arrival in Geneva. One was George Bell's *Christianity and World Order*. Bonhoeffer could hardly be surprised at the tone sounded by his most important ecumenical friend but he was overwhelmingly grateful to find his wise, firm and generous commitment to justice, peace and the reconciling mission of the universal church being reaffirmed as strongly in wartime as before. Bell was in no doubt that Hitler must be defeated but refused to call the war "holy" or "Christian" and still called for any genuine opportunity for a just, negotiated peace not to be missed. Most strikingly of all Bonhoeffer read the sentence about the responsibility of the universal church: "It cannot . . . be wrong for Christians in one belligerent country to seek such opportunities as may be open, to discover through neutral channels, in every way possible from fellow-Christians in another belligerent country, what terms of peace would be likely to create a lasting peace, and not lead to a further poisoning of international relationships." This was exactly why Bonhoeffer was in Geneva. Visser't Hooft told Bonhoeffer that his English friend was already facing hostility from some sections of British opinion that had read such remarks and heard of his speeches in the House of Lords, and were demanding to know what substance if any there could be to such hopes.

The second book was William (Bill) Paton's *The Church and the New Order*, published by the SCM Press in July that year. Paton, a Presbyterian, had succeeded Joe Oldham as general secretary of the International Missionary Council in 1938 and was also now the World Council's associate secretary in London. He was moreover leader of the Peace Aims Group that had been formed by the WCC and the World Alliance just before the outbreak of war, and which via Geneva was seeking to maintain communication with opposition circles in Germany. The book is similar in vein to Bell's, most evidently in highlighting the debate about "peace aims" that was underway in Britain. An important stimulus had come from Pope Pius XII who in

William Paton

December 1940 had issued his famous "five peace points". But the debate was taken up in a specifically British way. On 21 December 1940, the London *Blitz* still raging, there appeared in the *Times* a letter signed by the archbishops of Canterbury and York (Cosmo Gordon Lang and William Temple respectively), the Roman Catholic Cardinal Hinsley and the moderator of the Free Church Council (W.H. Armstrong). For those times it was a remarkably ecumenical initiative. They reaffirmed the Pope's five points: the right to life and independence of every nation in justice and reciprocity; deliverance from slavery to the armaments race; the need for a juridical institution to guarantee observance of treaties and conditions of peace; a European settlement involving revision of treaties regarded by some parties as inherently unjust; and a passion for adherence to the values and spirit of the Christian ideal of justice as proclaimed in the Sermon on the Mount. Based on these principles the church leaders called for inequalities of wealth to be abolished, equal opportunities for education for children regardless of race or class, safeguarding of the family, restoring the sense of divine vocation to work, and – prophetically in view of today's continuing travails – that "the resources of the earth should be used as

God's gifts to the whole human race, and used with due consideration for the needs of the present and future generations."

Paton, as Bell, uplifted all this, and also paid warm tribute to the Confessing Church. But Paton's book also differed in some ways. He attempted to be more specific about the likely future course of the world during and after the war, seeing the key to a future of justice, freedom and human rights as firmly in the conjoined hands of Britain and the USA – Russia hardly features on his horizon at all except as a problem to itself. (It should be noted that Paton was writing before Hitler's onslaught on Russia was launched, setting in train the military story that would inexorably bring the Soviet Union onto the world stage as a super-power, and several months before the Japanese attack on Pearl Harbor in December that would bring the USA into the war.) He was also clear that the moral, as well as physical, chaos that had been brought to Europe could not be cleared up overnight. In addition, Paton drew upon a wide selection of contemporary British sources. So Bonhoeffer could read extensive extracts from his old friend Joe Oldham's writings in the *Christian Newsletter* (there were full copies in Geneva) and its associated books; also John Middleton Murray, Lord Halifax, Arnold Toynbee and others, and was also referred back to material from the 1937 Oxford conference. This was a liberating discovery for someone who already felt a prisoner in the totalitarian isolation of his homeland. Just as Bell, Paton, Oldham and their friends were calling for recognition that there was "another Germany" to that of Hitler, so Bonhoeffer could take back firm evidence to his colleagues that there was "another Britain" to that portrayed by the regime's propaganda machine – and sometimes by the official declarations from Britain itself.

But Bonhoeffer had questions to raise and some criticisms to make that Visser't Hooft also saw as important. Together they wrote a substantial comment on Paton's book. First they made clear their admiration and gratitude for his basic line that the church did have a ministry to the public realm, consisting in reminding the nations of the abiding commandments and realities which must be taken seriously if there is to be a new, true order and if another divine judgment is to be avoided. Realistically but hopefully they stated:

> We are deeply grateful that there has grown up a community of Christians of different nations which can undertake this task as a common task. We have good reason to hope that that community will come out of this war as an even more united body than it was before the war. Those who are conscious

of their membership in this body are as yet a small group, but they are never-theless not unimportant, because they are practically the only international community which remains united in spite of war and conflict.

They agree that Germany must accept disarmament, but argue that this should not be stated as the main peace aim "as is being done too often" but as part of a much wider programme including "the giving of a certain amount of political and economic security to a disarmed Germany, and the acceptance by all nations of a certain supra-national control of their armaments." Further, they say, Paton's description of the "chaos behind the war" has not gone to the heart of the moral confusion of Germany that lies in Nazism's ability to present to Germans an injus-tice as justice. There was *just enough* "relative justice" in some of Germany's post-Versailles claims to allow Hitler to project himself as the prophet who came to re-establish justice. Hence it has become difficult for the German nation to under-stand the true character of the regime.

And so on. But the most telling paragraph is that which questions whether Paton's vision of the future, based on "rights" does adequate justice to the role of *law*:

The Anglo-Saxon world summarizes the struggle against the omnipotence of the State in the word 'freedom'. And Paton gives us a charter of human 'rights and liberties' which are to provide the norm of action by the State. But these expressions must, as Paton indicates, 'be translated into terms which relate them more closely to the life of other peoples.' For freedom is too negative a word to be used in a situation where *all* order has been destroyed. And liberties are not enough when men seek first of all for some minimum security. These words remind too much of the old liberalism which because of its failures is itself largely responsible for the development towards State absolutism.

Post-war Germany may well, therefore, be in need for some time of a more authori-tarian structure of government than the Anglo-Saxons envisage. The interim measures are therefore important, and they feel that neither Paton, nor Oldham, have yet shed sufficient light on this problem.

Then to a point of crucial importance for the "other Germany". What terms of peace? The total disarmament and occupation of Germany would make it well night impossible to create a new German government. "Would not those groups which are definitely anti-Nazi feel that even Hitler was better than this complete collapse of German integrity?" What follows is exactly what Bonhoeffer was sent to ask on behalf of the resistance:

> The question must then be faced whether it is possible to offer such terms of peace to Germany that a new government composed of non-Nazi German leaders who are ready for international collaboration may not be discredited from the outside in the eyes of their own people. Or to put it the other way round . . . whether a German government which makes a complete break with Hitler and all he stands for can hope to get such terms of peace that it has some chance to survive.

Finally there is a warning that Bolshevism too, unless the war calls forth funda-mental changes in the Russian state "may well become a tremendous menace to all countries which have been betting on the wrong horse and which will find their Fascist systems discredited by a German defeat."

Visser't Hooft sent the paper to Hugh Martin, editor of the SCM Press in London, and it was shared with the Peace Aims Group. Some members evidently sought to interest influential figures on the fringes of government, but the substantial and considered reply that had been hoped for did not come. (Paton himself was to die in the autumn of 1942, a major loss to the whole ecumenical movement). Of course authorship of the paper was kept anonymous and that may have added to doubts about the significance of the ideas in it. But the essay is a classic and moving case of an attempt at ecumenical dialogue across the battle-lines, of the search for common lines of action when all else seems to be falling apart. Nothing was more urgent in what Bonhoeffer and Visser't Hoof wrote than their plea that more of the kind of thinking that Paton, Bell, Oldham and others were presenting should be made known in and to Germany: "Why does the BBC say so little about those things?"

During the following months the situation of the resistance circle with which Bonhoeffer was linked grew still more problematic as the basic question remained unanswered: if Hitler was overthrown would a non-Nazi government have the chance to negotiate a peace, or would Germany, regardless of who was in power, be forced into unconditional surrender? The only hope would seem to lie in convinc-ing the British and their allies of the reality of an opposition in Germany that could both carry out the overthrow and constitute a government totally different from Hitler's. When Bonhoeffer went on his third visit to Geneva in May 1942 he had no idea that this task of communication was about to land on his own shoulders in an unprecedented way. Soon after he arrived he heard that George Bell was at that

The house on Stora Gatan, Sigtuna, where Bonhoeffer met with George Bell, May 1942

very moment visiting church leaders in neutral Sweden. Realizing the opportunity this could present he hurried back to Berlin and consulted with Colonel Beck, a leading military figure in the resistance, and with von Dohnanyi. It was agreed he should go. Three days later, in great secrecy and armed with a pass from the foreign ministry he was on the plane to Stockholm. He arrived on 31 May and learned that Bell was in fact in Sigtuna, the small town just north of the city. Sigtuna, nestling along the shore of the beautiful lake Mälaren, claims to be the oldest medieval town in Sweden. Picturesque wooden houses line the oldest street, Stora Gatan, and it was in one of these that Bell was staying as a guest of Manfred Bjornquist, director of the famous evangelical academy there.

Bell was informed he had a visitor, and could not contain first his astonishment and then his delight when Dietrich Bonhoeffer walked into the room. But Bonhoeffer was not the only one to have come to see Bell. Hans Schönfeld had also come from Geneva and had already briefed Bell with at least some of the same information that Bonhoeffer wanted to share. It seems that Bonhoeffer had known that Schönfeld would be visiting Bell but they had travelled quite independently. It is likely that by himself Schönfeld, whose somewhat compromising stance during the earlier Church Struggle had made him an object of some suspicion, would not have been able to convince Bell completely. Bonhoeffer's arrival however left him in no doubt that a real and urgent message was forthcoming from the German opposition. In private, and at great length, Bonhoeffer gave him the full picture of the scale of that opposition: the conspiracy aiming at total destruction of the Hitler regime and its instruments of terror; the supporters of the resistance in the army and state administration, former trades unionists etc; its aims of renouncing aggression, repeal of all Nazi legislation, withdrawing German forces from occupied lands, ending support from Japan, co-operating with the Allies in reconstruction . . . and so on. He gave Bell actual names of the chief figures involved, of whose reliability he was in no doubt.

Bell was impressed not just by what Bonhoeffer had to say but by the way he said it. In a memorable utterance shortly after the war he recalled:

> Of these last solemn talks I had with Dietrich I will say nothing further but this: Deeply committed as he was to the plan for elimination, he was not altogether at ease about such a solution. 'There must be punishment by God,' he said. 'We do not want to escape repentance.' The elimination itself, he urged, must be understood as an act of repentance. 'Oh, we have to be punished. Christians do not wish to escape repentance or chaos, if God wills to bring it on us. We must endure this judgment as Christians.' Very moving was our talk: very moving our farewell. And the last letter I had from him, just before he returned to Berlin, knowing what might well await him there, I shall treasure for the whole of my life.

So took place one of the most poignant ecumenical encounters of the war and indeed of the whole modern ecumenical story. Bell promised to convey what he had heard not just to intimate colleagues in London but to the highest circles of the British government. As a senior bishop and member of the House of Lords his admittance to such circles could hardly be gainsaid. But he warned both Bonhoeffer and Schönfeld he could not promise results. Militarily the war was at a very critical phase. Even supposing sympathy from the British government, it would have been hazardous for Britain to be seen by her American and Russian allies to be suing for peace with an untried opposition in Germany. Nevertheless procedures were worked out for the coming weeks and a system of coded communication via Geneva agreed upon.

Bell returned to England and, as is well known, in a memorandum and in a personal meeting with foreign secretary Anthony Eden presented the case he had heard in Sigtuna. In particular, it was asked whether allied governments would treat with a new bona fide German government along the lines indicated by Bonhoeffer and Schönfeld, and would they announce publicly and clearly that, once Hitler and the whole regime had been removed, they would be prepared to negotiate with a new German government that renounced aggression and pledged a policy of peacemaking as stated in Sigtuna? He also saw Sir Stafford Cripps, a member of the cabinet, who was sympathetic and who had also met with Visser't Hooft on one of his visits to London. Cripps promised to speak supportively to Eden. But Eden's eventual reply was negative. Relations with the other allies in war seemed determinative, and to hard-headed political leaders there still seemed too little visibility of the "opposition" in Germany. Through 1942 and into 1943 Bell went public as far as he was able without betraying the figures in the resistance, by writing in Oldham's *Christian Newsletter* and by speaking in the House of Lords on the need to take seriously the possibility of an opposition in Germany; pressing the view that a movement which entirely repudiated Nazism deserved to be a partner in negotiation as an alternative to the total annihilation of the country. Further talks with Eden took place, but to no avail. The eventual message to Geneva was therefore disappointing. The resisters were left effectively on their own.

Meanwhile, time was running out for Bonhoeffer and those members of his family involved in the resistance. He had evaded military service for too long, and the suspicions about "Operation 7" needed answering. On 5 April 1943 both he and Hans von Dohnanyi were arrested. Bonhoeffer was put in Tegel military prison, Berlin. That would be his home for the next eighteen months.

CHAPTER 6

FROM TEGEL TO FLOSSENBÜRG
1943-45

Tegel is a district in north-west Berlin, most well-known today as the site of Berlin's main international airport. The visitor landing there can easily spot to the north of the runway (the opposite side to the terminal building) the twin conical towers of what was the Tegel military prison and is now a high security psychiatric institution.

Imprisonment was undoubtedly, in its earliest phase, a tormenting experience for Dietrich Bonhoeffer. Beset by loneliness, anxiety for himself and those close to him, and the sheer uncertainty of his fate, he had to draw upon all his resources to find a new wholeness of living. That he did so through prayer and meditation; through renewed study and reflection and through finding ways of being helpful to those around him – fellow prisoners and even his warders – is the great testimony of his prison writings, now figuring among the world's spiritual and intellectual classics. Not that he was initially in great mortal danger. The Nazi regime had scarcely any inkling as yet of the actual conspiracy against Hitler being plotted by Oster, Canaris, von Dohnanyi and their circle. The charges being brought against Bonhoeffer related to his continued evasion of military service and suspicions about "Operation 7". The interrogations and legal processes dragged on inconclusively through 1943 and into 1944, which only added to Bonhoeffer's sense of frustration. Only after the failed attempt on Hitler's life of 20 July 1944 did the situation change dramatically. For nearly all his time in Tegel Bonhoeffer had had permission to write to and receive letters from his parents, brothers and fiancée Maria von Wedemeyer, and at intervals to be visited by them and by Eberhard Bethge. The now famous correspondence with Eberhard Bethge that began in late 1943 was entirely clandestine, using the services of a friendly warder who acted as courier between Bonhoeffer and the family home in Berlin. It was from the end of April 1944 that those letters to Bethge launched into the startling explorations of "religion-less Christianity" in a "world come of age". But there were not only letters. Poetry, novel-writing and drama were among Bonhoeffer's new experiments at communicating his thoughts and feel-ings. Nor did he even, in a sense, give up preaching. Just over a month after his arrest he produced a sermon for the wedding of Eberhard Bethge and Renate Schleicher his niece, and in May the following year wrote a powerful medi-tation on the baptism of their son – his godson – Dietrich.

From behind the bars of the first-floor cell in Tegel, Sabine and her family and England obviously now seemed even further away. Dietrich had written to Sabine on each of his visits to neutral Switzerland and Sweden, and in 1942 she had been able to write to him enclosing pictures of his two nieces in their English school uniforms. In addition, George Bell was able to meet with the Leibholzes after the Sigtuna meeting. But once news came of the arrest all attempts at communica-tion had to cease. There could only be scraps of information out of Germany, mainly via Geneva. Eberhard Bethge, again ostensibly for official *Abwehr* purposes, was dispatched to Switzerland a few weeks after Bonhoeffer's arrest to inform the ecumenical contacts of what had happened. He brought back not only news in return (including the news of

Tegel: the view from Bonhoffer's cell

Bonhoeffer in the courtyard at Tegel Prison

William Paton's death) but a cigar from Karl Barth that soon filled cell 92 (and no doubt the corridor outside) with its fragrance.

Bonhoeffer's mental and spiritual survival in Tegel owed much to his insatiable desire to continue studying and learning, and to draw upon both his own rich past experiences and memories and upon the great world of thought that was still accessible to him. There was a good prison library, and his family were also able to obtain many books for him, whether theological, philosophical, historical or just good literature. Most of this was of course German, but the English world continued to draw him too. Once inside Tegel, one of the first books he asked his parents to bring from his bedroom in the Marienburgerallee was Edwyn Hoskyns' *The Riddle of the New Testament* (1931), a somewhat surprising choice given that the source-critical approach to the Bible had not normally been a subject that excited him. It might possibly have been pre-arranged to request this book as one of those to be used to convey secret information back, since the family conspirators used the method of marking books with a minute dot under one letter on one page at a time to spell out a message relating to the interrogations. (If this had been the case, the title of the book would have been ironically very apt.) Or it may simply be that he wished to keep up his English. In a later letter to his parents he wrote that his daily routine included a study of English grammar "about which I can still learn all kinds of things". To Eberhard Bethge he reported reading, of all things, a history of Scotland Yard (one trusts he was not hoping to get clues on how his interrogators might behave) but he was still more excited about "a gigantic English novel which goes from 1500 to today, by Hugh Walpole, written in 1909" – this was of course *The Herries Chronicle*. Bonhoeffer always relished the continuity of a rich tradition as an essential ingredient in the wholeness of life, a continuity that he felt had now been savagely broken in his own country.

In a letter to Eberhard Bethge in December 1943 Bonhoeffer reflects on a theme that had always been important to him: the danger of too much openness about one's own feelings such as fear, and of too much inquisitiveness about the inner life of other people. "After all, 'truthfulness' does not mean uncovering everything that exists." In a fallen, sinful word there must be reticence and secrecy about certain matters, and a desire to "expose" everything under the guise of "exceptional honesty" is cynical and harmful. God made clothes for the fallen first pair to wear. He then asks: "But is not this somewhat akin to the so-called English 'hypocrisy', which we contrast with German 'honesty'? I believe we Germans have never properly grasped the meaning of 'concealment', i.e. what is in the end the *status corruptionis* of the world." Interestingly, Sabine Leibholz was at the same time making this same discovery in English life and manners:

> . . . I was interested to notice that in England people avoid burdening each other with accounts of their physical condition. Illness is hardly ever spoken of. It is not a fit subject for discussion . . . A certain distance was maintained between individuals, since 'familiarity breeds contempt' and this applied to almost all human relationships. Reason rather than emotion prevails, and one never exacerbates an emotional situation . . . One should never be interfering and should occupy oneself solely with one's own affairs. There were postcards bearing the words 'Do someone a good turn every day – leave them alone!'

Of course many British (English at any rate) people take slight amusement at being seen as the race of the stiff upper lip. Equally, everyone in Britain knows examples of the person who *does* take delight in talking at length and in greatest detail about their interesting physical condition. But the notion of reticence, of distance between people, that Dietrich and Sabine had both appreciated in England (did they perhaps talk about this during their times together in London?) is a good instance of Bonhoeffer empathizing with a feature of a culture other than his own and seeing its potential significance. Closely allied to it is his recognition of the proper element of *mystery* in relation both to God and to other humans that becomes an important element in his distinction between faith and "religion". It was in London, in his Trinity Sunday sermon of 1934 (see page 70) that he had first spoken of the greatest mystery being the person closest to us. Now in prison, working out his new theology, he writes "The beyond is not what is infinitely remote, but what is nearest at hand" and "The transcendental is not infinite and unattainable tasks, but the neighbour who is within reach in any given situation." Religion, Bonhoeffer argues in his later letters, seeks to manipulate God, either by first banishing God beyond the everyday world and then bringing God in as a last resort, or trying to exploit the divine for self-centred ends. Equally, religion attempts to manipulate people into believing that they need such a stop-gap God. Faith, like Jesus, lets God be God and allows other people to be as they present themselves to be, and the mystery of both the divine and the human to be preserved in a real encounter in this world.

Quite apart from his calm reflections on "Englishness", from late November 1943 Bonhoeffer was confronted with another kind of experience of the United Kingdom, as he and everyone in Berlin received almost nightly visits from several hundred young men from Britain and the Commonwealth. Having earlier in the year laid waste much of the Ruhr and fire-bombed Hamburg, the chief of RAF Bomber Command, Arthur Harris, decided to direct his formidable squadrons of Lancasters and Halifaxes against the German capital and, in his own words, "wreck Berlin from end to end". The first raid took place on the night of 16/17 November but although over 400 aircraft took part the damage was relatively moderate. The next raid on the

night of 22/23 November brought nearly 800 aircraft over Berlin and the effect was devastating, as it was the following night also. Even Joseph Goebbels was awed as he recorded in his diary "Hell itself seems to have broken loose over us", with high explosives raining down, many government buildings ablaze, and the sky garishly alight with parachute flares, searchlight beams and flak. The raids were to continue into the early months of 1944.

Bonhoeffer's Advent visitors: RAF crews at debriefing after the raid on Berlin of 22/23 November 1943

For a time, therefore, Bonhoeffer was in far more immediate danger from the British than from the Gestapo and SS. Tegel was close by the large Borsig engineering works that made the area a prime target; the safety of prisoners, many of whom were very young soldiers being held on minor charges, was not a top priority for the authorities. On the morning of 23 November Bonhoeffer wrote, somewhat understatedly, to Eberhard Bethge, "Tonight's raid was not exactly pleasant" and the same day he made out a new will and sent Bethge directions for arrangements in the event of his death. On the night of 26/27 November Borsig was hit heavily. Most prisoners had to endure the ordeal still locked in their cells, screaming for help, and many were injured. Bonhoeffer joined the first-aid team: "we had finished bandaging them by one o'clock." From his own cell window he had had a grandstand view of the attack: "It really is a strange feeling, to see the 'Christmas trees', the flares that the leading aircraft drops, coming right down over our heads."

This was just before Advent Sunday. Did Bonhoeffer, perhaps, recall his first Advent sermon in London in 1933 (see page 68) when he had spoken of the helplessness of the prisoner who can only wait and hope for deliverance from outside? The sight of the RAF pathfinder flares – those "Christmas trees" as the Berliners called them – descending towards him could only have increased that sense. As far as the

'Christmas trees': RAF bombers release their flares over the target area

moral aspects of the bombing were concerned, Bonhoeffer was very restrained. Back in England in his courageous speeches in the House of Lords George Bell had been protesting about the carpet bombing of German cities as a violation of just war principles. Bonhoeffer is silent on this nor does he call it, as did many Germans, "terror bombing". On the other hand neither does he speak of it simplistically as God's judgment on Germany. To Eberhard Bethge he confines himself to saying positively:

> The fact that the horrors of war are now coming home to us with such force will no doubt, if we survive, provide us with the necessary basis for making it possible to reconstruct the life of the nations, both spiritually and materially, on Christian principles. So we must try to keep these experiences in our minds, use them in our work, make them bear fruit, and not just shake them off. Never have we been so plainly conscious of the wrath of God, and that is a sign of his grace.

At the immediate level Bonhoeffer was far more concerned about the treatment of prisoners during the raids and wrote a report to the prison authorities on practical steps that he thought could be taken for both their physical and psychological welfare. But it is characteristic of him that he was able to act in the here and now and at the same time to reflect on the longer term significance of what was happening. Taking his cue from that terrible night sky over Berlin the English scholar and poet Geoffrey Hill strikingly confronts us with Bonhoeffer, and his abiding relevance, in his poem "Christmas Trees":

> Bonhoeffer in his skylit cell
> bleached by the flares' candescent fall,
> pacing out his own citadel,
> restores the broken themes of praise,
> encourages our borrowed days,
> by logic of his sacrifice.
>
> Against wild reasons of the state
> his words are quiet but not too quiet.
> We hear too late or not too late.

One consequence of the air raids, and about which Bonhoeffer probably had mixed feelings, was that the papers relating to his case were lost when the judge-advocate's office was hit, adding to the delays. Nothing conclusive happened as winter wore on into spring 1944. Meanwhile Eberhard Bethge was now in army uniform (the best camouflage for those in the resistance) and was posted to a unit in Italy. Bonhoeffer ensured that he had the addresses of George Bell ("Uncle George" he was referred to in code) and other contacts in Britain in case he was taken prisoner. For himself, Bonhoeffer remained hopeful of a favorable outcome to his case should it ever actually come to court. But then came 20 July 1944 and the failure of Claus von Stauffenberg's bomb attack on Hitler, the final, fateful culmination of the whole conspiracy. Bonhoeffer knew that whatever the previous charges, his own fate would now likely be sealed. His letter written next day to Bethge is his finest testament of faith, of accepting the way of sharing the sufferings of God in the world, a way that is yet full of gratitude and hope.

It was only at the end of September when at Zossen, not far from Berlin, files directly incriminating Dohnanyi and his circle were found and the real peril began. Bonhoeffer was moved from Tegel to the Gestapo cellars in Prinz-Albrecht-Strasse in the centre of Berlin, joining Colonel Oster and other military leaders of the conspiracy. By now Bonhoeffer's brother Klaus and his brother-in-law Rüdiger Schleicher were also imprisoned, and soon so too was Eberhard Bethge who was brought back from Italy under armed escort. By now visits and letters were at a minimum. Compared to Tegel Prinz-Albrecht-Strasse was hell. The interrogations were brutal, although it seems that Bonhoeffer himself was not actually tortured. Klaus Bonhoeffer did suffer that fate, and Hans von Dohnanyi was atrociously treated during a long illness. Yet it was in those cellars that Bonhoeffer, at New Year 1945, wrote for Maria von Wedemeyer the poem whose English version now features in many English-language hymnbooks as *By gracious powers, so wonderfully sheltered*. Then at the begin-

ning of February Bonhoeffer was transferred south to Buchenwald concentration camp, close by Weimar. By now the family had no news of his whereabouts. Maria von Wedemeyer, trudging through the snows, made a fruitless tour of prison camps seeking information about him. They knew more, but still not enough, about the others in the

Buchenwald

family: Klaus Bonhoeffer and Rüdiger Schleicher had been condemned to death by the notorious "People's Court" early in the new year, but as to their actual fate, their relatives were in the dark.

At Buchenwald Bonhoeffer found himself in an air-raid shelter serving as a makeshift prison, shared by a group of inmates that included a Russian air-force officer and two Englishmen, Hugh Falconer and Payne Best. Falconer was an RAF squadron-leader who had been captured in an undercover operation in Tunisia in 1941, trying to land with a radio set from a motor-boat. Payne Best, a captain in military intelligence, had spent nearly the whole of the war in prison camps, having been seized in November 1939 on the Dutch border during an attempt to spirit a senior officer who had claimed to be working against Hitler out of Germany. Best was seen by some prisoners as the very model of the international caricature of the English gentleman: tall, gaunt (stooping a little through emaciation), even after years in prison sporting a check jacket and flannel trousers – and a monocle, not to mention a somewhat horsy grin thanks to outsize false teeth supplied by the camp doctor

Captain Payne Best

at Sachsenhausen. An "obliging smile and trustworthy discretion" completed the picture. But Best was no P.G. Wodehouse creation. He was quite capable of having blistering rows with warders and even on occasion with SS guards. His account of his capture and all his subsequent experiences as a prisoner is told in graphic (and often highly entertaining) detail in his book *The Venlo Incident*, and it is to him and Falconer that we owe such pictures as we have of Bonhoeffer during his last days. The fact that both men saw him just as he was, without knowing anything about his previous life or background nor anticipating the aura and fame that would subsequently attach to him, makes their impressions all the more telling.

Best and Falconer naturally spent as much time as possible together, cheerfully sharing (or competing for) their tobacco rations. They soon discovered that prisoner

Bonhoeffer was unfailingly generous with his supply. And he clearly welcomed the chance to speak English again after such a long time. Best and Falconer had the impression that most of the German prisoners seemed to distrust each other. But Bonhoeffer shared a cell with General Friedrich von Rabenau, a military historian and lay theologian, and Falconer noticed that they were the only two who seemed to get on well together, often engaging in lively theological debate. Best saw in Rabenau the "militant churchman" who expects, like the general he was, unquestioning obedience to his views. By contrast, Bonhoeffer:

> . . . was all humility and sweetness; he always seemed to me to diffuse an atmosphere of happiness, of joy in every smallest event in life, and of deep gratitude for the mere fact that he was alive. There was something dog-like in the look of fidelity in his eyes and of gladness if you showed that you liked him. He was one of the very few men that I have ever met to whom his God was real and ever close to him.

And Hugh Falconer in a reminiscence for a BBC radio programme similarly recalled:

> He stood out from other prisoners by his look of serenity and obviously unshakeable faith, and I suppose for that reason not really worried about what was going to happen to him because of a complete certainty that whatever was going to happen to him was what God wanted to happen to him and that was therefore what he wanted too.

But days passed slowly. Life at Buchenwald was cold, hungry, frequently punctuated by air-raids and with no opportunity for exercise except walking up and down the short corridor between the cells. Bonhoeffer was touched when Payne Best gave him a chess set that enabled him once again to indulge one of his favourite pastimes. But some kind of end was clearly in sight. On 1 April – Easter Sunday – the sound of tank guns and artillery could be heard: the Americans were at the river Werra some 40 miles to the south-west.

Buchenwald's days were numbered. On 3 April, sixteen prisoners, including Best, Falconer, Bonhoeffer, Rabenau and two women were squeezed into a stinking, wood-fired prison van that left Buchenwald and headed south. Best describes it as a hell of a journey, with continual stops for refueling with wood. "There was no light, we had noting to eat or drink nor, but for the generosity of Bonhoeffer who, although a smoker, had saved up his scanty ration of tobacco and now insisted in contributing

Flossenbürg: the execution yard

to the common good, anything to smoke. He was a good and saintly man." The excruciatingly painful journey lasted all night, relieved by only one comfort stop to answer the call of nature, and by Falconer's practical skill in re-stowing the baggage to make some more space. There was fear that they were heading for Flossenbürg, the extermination camp in Bavaria and indeed on the outskirts of nearby Weiden they were stopped by police and three of the prisoners' names were called out. They were never seen again. The night was spent in Regensburg. Next day the van was lurching further southwards when the steering broke down. The ever-practical Falconer, a trained engineer, confirmed there was no way of repairing it there and then. A message was sent back to Regensburg and eventually a "magnificent bus, all big plate glass windows and soft upholstered seats" appeared and the journey continued in what now seemed luxurious comfort. In the evening they reached Schönberg, a pretty village set among the rolling green slopes and woods of the Bayerischer Wald. A school

Schönberg

building (today it's a massage-parlour) served as makeshift accommodation for the party. With windows opened to the glorious spring countryside surrounding them, now apparently so far south as to be out of harm's way, and amid all the breakdown in communications that was accompanying the military collapse, hopes were rising for survival. There was almost a party atmosphere with jokes, pranks and for once nearly enough to eat. Unbeknown to them, however, in Berlin Hitler had finally ordered the elimination of both Dietrich Bonhoeffer and Hans von Dohnanyi, and some telephones still worked.

Low Sunday, 8 April, the first Sunday after Easter, dawned. Not on his initiative but at the request of some of the other prisoners, most of whom were Catholics, Bonhoeffer conducted a short service including a sermon based on the texts for the day; Isaiah 55:1 and 1 Peter 1:3, verses that combine to affirm the redemptive sufferings of Christ and the resurrection from the dead. Hugh Falconer, again, recalled:

> The text of the sermon, I remember, was "By his sufferings are we healed." And the main theme he drew from this was not that we could in any way rely on God to answer prayers for our specific release and return to our families, but rather for the assurance of salvation. And I particularly remember that one hymn we sang was *Ein' feste Burg ist unser Gott.*

Payne Best says: ". . . Pastor Bonhoeffer held a little service and spoke to us in a manner which reached the hearts of all, finding just the right words to express the spirit of our imprisonment and the thoughts which it had brought."

But he had hardly finished his last prayer when "the door opened and two evil-looking men in civilian clothes came in and said, 'Prisoner Bonhoeffer. Get ready to come with us'." Everyone knew what that meant. Surrounded by goodbyes, Bonhoeffer quickly drew Best aside, saying, "This is the end, for me the beginning of life." He just had time to give him a message to pass, if possible, to Bishop George Bell: ". . . a friend to all evangelical pastors in Germany . . . Tell him that with him I believe in the reality of our Christian brotherhood that rises above all national conflicts and interests and that our victory is certain."

Dietrich Bonhoeffer's last known words were thus spoken, in English, to an Englishman and for a Christian friend in England, but they are a legacy for the whole community of faith. At Flossenbürg where he was now taken, his words were few as he faced the final court-martial that night. He apparently offered no defence,

Flossenbürg: memorial to the resisters executed 9 April 1945

having said and done enough in his life. Next morning came for him the end and the beginning, as he was hanged along with Admiral Canaris, Colonel Oster, General von Rabenau and four others. Hans von Dohnanyi was executed the same day at Sachsenhausen. At Flossenbürg, the memorial plaque that now stands near where the gallows stood is inscribed 2 Timothy 1:7: For God did not give us a spirit of cowardice, but rather a spirit of power and of love and of self-discipline.

CHAPTER 7

SORROW AND THANKSGIVING

In London and all over Britain there was dancing in the streets and parties were held for the children as a relieved and thankful people celebrated "VE-Day" on 8 May. In Germany there was utter desolation and chaos. For weeks news travelled slowly, if at all. Berlin was totally cut off. Such information as there was about those who had or had not survived Hitler's final revenge in many cases reached the outside world more quickly than it was heard in Germany itself. Not until the very end of May did the Bonhoeffer family receive confirmation that Klaus Bonhoeffer and Rüdiger Schleicher had been executed. About Dietrich they had no news whatever, and could only fear. It was in fact at about the same time that a telegram reached Geneva from two survivors, Josef Müller and Fabian von Schlabrendorff, that Klaus and Dietrich Bonhoeffer had met their end. Alfred Freudenberg, secretary for the refugee service at the World Council office, telegraphed Julius Rieger in London (he had remained as pastor there throughout the war). Next day Rieger telephoned the Leibholzes in Oxford and asked whether he could come and see them. When he arrived Sabine knew at once from his face that he was bringing dark tidings, confirmed only too well as he said, "It's Dietrich. He is no more – and Klaus too . . . ." Rieger gravely laid the telegram from Geneva on the table and then read from Matthew 10, one of the passages about faithfulness in persecution that Dietrich had expounded so powerfully in his *Discipleship*. But the Leibholz family, having waited and hoped so long for a reunion in a new Germany, were grief-stricken.

George Bell was visiting New York with Visser't Hooft at the time and received the news by cable. Deeply pained by the losses himself, on his return to England he sought to bring what consolation he could to the Leibholzes. But it was already apparent that the deaths of Dietrich and the other family members had a significance going beyond a purely private grief. After consulting with the Leibholzes, Bell together with Julius Rieger and Franz Hildebrandt, who had been serving as pastor to German refugees in Cambridge, organized a memorial service for Dietrich and Klaus. It was held on 27 July in Holy Trinity Church, Kingsway, in central

Holy Trinity Church, Kingsway

London (the church is now a deconsecrated building). It fell at a significant time, just when people in Britain were coping with the images of bestiality from the liberated death-camps and a new demonization of everything and everyone German might be expected. Yet the church was crowded to the doors as many Londoners joined the Leibholz family; members of the London German congregations and other sympathizers. Moreover, the service was broadcast by the BBC and transmitted on its German service.

Julius Rieger conducted the service for the friend whom he had first welcomed to London back in 1933. The great congregation rose for the opening hymn: *For all the saints who from their labours rest.* Then Rieger opened a prayer with the bidding:

> We are gathered here in the presence of God, to make thankful remembrance of the life and work of his servant Dietrich Bonhoeffer who – together with his brother Klaus Bonhoeffer – gave his life in faith and obedience to his holy word, to thank God for his gifts which were his by God's grace, for his use of those gifts in the service of the universal church, and for his courage, wisdom and friendship which have strengthened and guided so many in the following of Christ.

The service was indeed being heard in Germany, and with no more profound effect than in the Marienburgerallee in Berlin where the radio had by pure chance been switched on at the start of the broadcast. It came as the confirmation of what Karl and Paula Bonhoeffer and their remaining family had been waiting, and fearing, to hear. This time, Dietrich would not be coming home.

There followed the litany of thanksgiving, some hymns sung in German including the Advent chorale *Wachet auf! Ruft uns die Stimme*, and a lesson from that same passage which Rieger had read to the Leibholzes when he brought the fateful news, Matthew 10:17-42.

Then came the sermon, preached by George Bell. It was Bell at his greatest in eloquent simplicity, every word weighted to convey deep feeling but without histrionics. He outlined Dietrich Bonhoeffer's life and career and movingly told of his last encounter with him in Sweden in 1942 when Bonhoeffer had not only informed him about the resistance but shared his own anguish at Germany's shame (see page 118). The last two paragraphs deserve to be quoted in full, for they continue to speak as powerfully to the church and Europe of today as they did then:

> And now Dietrich has gone. He died, with his brother, as a hostage. Our debt to them, and to all others similarly murdered, is immense. His death is a death for Germany – indeed for Europe too. He made the sacrifice of human prospects, of home, friends, and career because he believed in God's vocation for his country, and refused to follow those false leaders, who were the servants of the devil. He was inspired by his faith in the living God, and by his devotion to truth and honour. And so his death, like his life, marks a fact of the deepest value in the witness of the Confessional Church. As one of a noble company of martyrs of differing traditions, he represents both the resistance of the believing soul, in the name of God, to the assault of evil, and also the moral and political revolt of the human conscience against injustice and cruelty. He and his fellows are indeed laid upon the foundation of the

Apostles and the Prophets. And it was this passion for justice that brought him, and so many others in the Confessional Church who were in agreement with him, into such close partnership with other resisters who, though outside the Church, shared the same humanitarian and liberal ideals.

Our Lord said, 'Except a grain of wheat fall into the ground and die, it abideth alone; but if it die, it bringeth forth much fruit. He that loveth his life shall lose it, and he that hateth his life in this world shall keep it unto life eternal.' To our earthly view Dietrich is dead. Deep and unfathomable as our sorrow seems, let us comfort one another with these words. For him and Klaus, and for the countless multitudes of their fellow victims through these terrible years of war, there is the resurrection from the dead: for Germany redemption and resurrection, if God please to lead the nation through men animated by his spirit: for the Church, not only in that Germany which he loved, but the Church Universal which was greater to him than nations, the hope of a new life. 'The blood of the martyrs is the seed of the Church.'

Franz Hildebrandt then preached in German, and after prayers of intercession and the closing hymn *Jerusalem, du hochgebaute Stadt* Bell gave the blessing. The new career of Dietrich Bonhoeffer on earth had begun.

CHAPTER 8

A LEGACY IN BRITAIN

The memorial service in Holy Trinity Church was but the beginning of Dietrich Bonhoeffer's posthumous impact in Britain. In fact a tribute to him appeared in the *Christian Newsletter* even before the service took place. George Bell continued to draw attention to Bonhoeffer as a sign that there had indeed been "another Germany" and, moreover, that his life and witness would be a source of renewal for the world church. Within a few years the main works of Bonhoeffer, hitherto existing in German and known if at all by only a few specialists, began to make their way into English. First of the substantial works to appear was an abridged version of *The Cost of Discipleship* in 1948 with a memoir by Gerhard Leibholz and a foreword by George Bell (the complete edition did not appear until 1959). Many of the prison writings, edited by Eberhard Bethge, first appeared in 1953 as *Letters and Papers from Prison*, followed by *Life Together* in 1954. The early, weighty philosophical-theological works came on the scene with *Act and Being* (1962) and *Sanctorum Communio* (1963). A first edition of *Ethics* appeared in 1955. In the course of the years Bonhoeffer featured in a succession of radio and television documentaries. His appeal in Britain, as in much of the rest of the English-speaking world, has been on several levels: as a prime witness that there was indeed "another Germany" and therefore powerfully encouraging the process of post-war reconciliation; as a creative theologian provoking new questions about the meaning of Christian faith in a "world come of age"; and as an inspiring example, both to the churches and to countless individuals, of what it means "to live for others" in the face of injustice.

In the story of the first wave of dissemination and interpretation of Bonhoeffer's work in Britain and the English-speaking world at large, two figures deserve special mention: Ronald Gregor Smith and Edwin Robertson. Gregor Smith was a Church of Scotland minister who, early on, acquired a remarkable command of German and while still a student in Edinburgh in 1937 produced the first English translation of Martin Buber's seminal *I and Thou*. After a wartime parish ministry in Selkirk and an army chaplaincy, he worked with the Allied Control Commission at Bonn university where he got to know Karl Barth and a number of other leading theologians in Germany. In 1947 he joined the SCM Press and took over as editor from Hugh Martin in 1950. It was on his initiative and under his editorship that many of the earliest Bonhoeffer translations were undertaken, and he continued his advocacy after he went to Glasgow university as professor of divinity in 1956. Along with Rudolf Bultmann, Paul Tillich and others Bonhoeffer became a vital ingredient in Gregor Smith's own ventures into in a theology for the contemporary world, as seen in his *The New Man* (1956) and *Secular Theology* (1966). His death in 1968 at the early age of 55 was a severe loss to the British theological scene.

Ronald Gregor Smith

Edwin Robertson is an English Baptist minister who, like Gregor Smith, served with the Control Commission in postwar Germany, not as an academic but as head of the Religious Affairs branch and with special responsibility for broadcasting, in Berlin. Like Gregor Smith he made close contact with the German theological scene including a number of Bonhoeffer's former students and colleagues. He returned to England in 1949 as assistant head of BBC Religious Broadcasting. He and Gregor Smith made an admirable team as broadcaster and academic publisher respectively and much of their theological output both in print and on

Edwin Robinson

the air concerned Bonhoeffer. Robertson subsequently worked successively for the United Bible Societies and the World Association for Christian Broadcasting (later Communication) and as a local church pastor. But even in such a busy life he began his own work of putting into English many of the letters, lectures, sermons and papers then being assembled by Eberhard Bethge in the collected writings of Bonhoeffer from the 1920s through to the period just before his imprisonment. Robertson's selections, translated by himself and John Bowden, appeared as *No Rusty Swords* (1963), *The Way to Freedom* (1972) and *True Patriotism* (1973) together with several monographs on Bonhoeffer. Now in his nineties and Pastor Emeritus of Heath Street Baptist Church, Hampstead, Edwin Robertson remains as enthusiastic an advocate of Bonhoeffer as ever.

In 1953 there arrived in London the person to whom more than anyone else the world owes its knowledge of Bonhoeffer and the preservation of his legacy. Eberhard Bethge, Bonhoeffer's closest friend in his last ten years and recipient of most of the prison letters, came to Sydenham to be pastor of the same congregation as his friend 20 years before. For the next eight years Forest Hill was home for him, his wife Renate (Bonhoeffer's niece) and their three children. The Bethges became particularly close friends of Ronald Gregor Smith and his German wife Käthe. In London Bethge continued assembling and editing Bonhoeffer's papers, but the pressures of a busy parish (and a conscientious pastoral commitment) delayed serious biographical work. There was moreover a particularly tangible contribution made by Bethge to ensure Bonhoeffer's continuing

Eberhard and Renate Bethge in retirement

visibility in London. Both St George's (Sydenham) and St Paul's (Aldgate) church buildings had been destroyed in the bombing of London. It was Bethge's initiative to have a completely new church built to a modern design at Sydenham. This opened on the original site in Dacres Road on 21 June 1959 as the Dietrich Bonhoeffer Church. In 1961 the Bethges returned to Germany, Eberhard taking responsibility as

At the opening of the new Dietrich Bonhoeffer Church, Sydenham, 21 June 1959

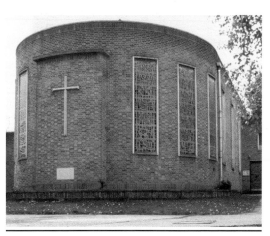

Dietrich Bonhoeffer Church, Sydenham, exterior and interior

Foundation stone of Dietrich Bonhoeffer Church, Sydenham, laid 20 July 1958

director of the pastoral training college at Rengsdorf bei Neuwied on the Rhine. Here there was more opportunity for scholarly pursuits and his monumental, definitive biography of Bonhoeffer appeared in German in 1967. An English slightly abridged edition appeared in 1970, the work of a team of translators under the editorship of Edwin Robertson. An earlier biography by the English author Mary Bosanquet, *The Life and Death of Dietrich Bonhoeffer*, had appeared in 1968. A revised and complete English edition of Bethge's biography was published by Fortress Press in 1999. Eberhard Bethge died in 2000.

Acknowledgment of Bonhoeffer's work, especially the implications of his prison writings on "religionless Christianity" for the form of faith in the contemporary world, was steadily progressing during the 1950s. As well as Ronald Gregor Smith, among the first to notice the importance of this was the now ageing Joe Oldham whose *Life is Commitment* (1953), drawing upon Bonhoeffer's prison writings before they were translated into English, must rank as one of the liveliest and provocative books ever written by a near-octogenarian. It was however exactly a decade later that something of a popular theological explosion occurred with the publication of *Honest to God* by John Robinson, then (1963) bishop of Woolwich. Robinson drew upon Bonhoeffer's "religionless Christianity", Bultmann's "demythologizing" of the New Testament message and Tillich's God as "Ground of Being" in his attack on the "God out there". Whether or not this recipe worked, the debate it unleashed about what it means to believe in God was unprecedented in modern Britain and, if nothing else, in being associated with the "new theology" Bonhoeffer became if not a household name then at least a church-door name almost overnight.

In the following decades, theological scholarship in Britain as in the USA and elsewhere has taken a more rounded view of Bonhoeffer, drawing upon the longer range of his life's work as the necessary interpretative background for his prison theology. While one cannot speak of a "Bonhoeffer school" in Britain a small but steady stream of British scholars in their doctoral theses and monographs have worked in their own way on Bonhoeffer, his thinking on ethics being a chief attraction. There is little sign of the "Bonhoeffer industry", as it is apt to be called by some, dying out. Each new generation seems to discover a new point of interest.

This is equally true at the more general level, where in the fields of ecumenism, mission, race relations and peacemaking Bonhoeffer remains a persistent challenge and inspiration, an inoculation against both the perennial temptation for Christians and churches to shut themselves away from the world and confine themselves to "religion" at the expense of the injustice and suffering around them, and the even more demonic tendency to use religion actually to sanction oppression and violence. For example, more than any other figure outside South Africa itself it was Dietrich Bonhoeffer who was repeatedly invoked in the British churches' involvement in the struggle against apartheid. And today, when religious overtones are again being heard in justifications of nationalism and war, and fundamentalisms are seeking political short-cuts to the kingdom of God on earth, it is Bonhoeffer who supplies one of the most vibrant nerves for prophetic resistance. To quote Geoffrey Hill again: "We hear too late or not too late."

This being recognized, we should not fear too much that Bonhoeffer might be reduced at a popular level to being a supplier of fill-in sermon quotes or epigrams for devotional diaries and calendars. In fact it is good that he should have a popular place among those recognized as the saints and martyrs of the church and accepted as a figure nourishing our faith and spirituality. It is good that the Sydenham manse (now converted to private flats) on Manor Mount today bears a "blue plaque" commemorating Bonhoeffer's residence

M. Liebholz-Bonhoeffer and Jim Dowd, Mayor of Lewisham, at the Blue Plaque unveiling

Westminster Abbey: Bonhoeffer stands between Archbishop Oscar Romero of El Salvador and Esther John (Qamar Zia) of Pakistan amidst the 20th century martyrs

there. It is good that he is included among the seven modern martyrs honoured in the Martyrs' Chapel in Canterbury Cathedral, dedicated in 1978, and who were specially commemorated during the visit of Pope John Paul II there in May 1982. It is good that his statue stands along with those of nine other 20th century martyrs above the entrance to the west door of Westminster Abbey. It was a telling moment when on 9 July 1998 those statues were unveiled in the presence of Queen Elizabeth II, for the church in Britain was acknowledging that in the 20th century the church worldwide had been called to live under the cross and could now literally look up to those who bore its weight. In the congregation that filled the abbey before the unveiling were Eberhard and Renate Bethge and their son Dietrich, Bonhoeffer's godson for whose baptism he had written from prison a sermon (see page 121). In those reflections Bonhoeffer hoped that: "Music, as your parents understand and practise it, will help to dissolve your perplexities and purify your character and sensibility and in times of care and sorrow will keep a ground-bass of joy alive in you." It was therefore a poignant and beautiful part of the service when Dietrich Bethge, now a professional cellist, played the sarabande from the Bach Suite in G. But that same baptismal sermon also contains a confession and warning: "Our church, which has been fighting in these years only for its self-preservation, as though that were an end in itself, is incapable of taking the word of reconciliation and redemption to mankind and the world."

Someone who said that can be welcomed as fully part of our home scene but never completely domesticated. Even George Bell could not always meet all his expectations. Britain and its churches had a great, irrefutable role in Bonhoeffer's life-story and have been important in its continuing outworking. But let every recollection of the Cambridge conference youth participant, of the London pastor, of the faithful ecumenical friend to George Bell and other British people, of the lover of so many things British even as British bombs were falling on him, be salted with the challenge of his simplest but most searching statement from prison: "The church is the church only when it exists for others."

Photograph Credits and Acknowledgements

Grateful acknowledgement and thanks are expressed to the individuals and organizations who have supplied the photographs listed below, and who have given permission for their use.

Chapter 1 A Scene in Berlin

P1 Dietrich Bonhoeffer 1930-31: (From *Dietrich Bonhoeffer. Bilder aus seinem Leben*, Munich: Chr. Kaiser Verlag 1986 [hereinafter referred to as *Bilder*] by permission of the editors, Renate Bethge and Christian Gremmels).

P4 Karl Barth: (World Council of Churches – WCC – Archives, Geneva)

P5 Franz Hildebrandt: (WCC Archives, Geneva)

Chapter 2 Cambridge 1931

P8 The Cambridge Backs: (Laura Clements)

P9 John Baillie: (WCC Archives, Geneva)

P10 Edward Arthur Burroughs, Bishop of Ripon: (Archival Service of the Diocese of Ripon)

P11 Trinity Great Court and Chapel: (Laura Clements)

P12 Ridley Hall: (Laura Clements)

P13 World Alliance garden party, Christ's College: (WCC Archives, Geneva)

P15 Procession to Great St Mary's for the closing service – the Danish contingent: (WCC Archives, Geneva)

P16 Great St Mary's: (Laura Clements)

Chapter 3 The London Pastor 1933-35

P18 Charles Freer Andrews: (SCM Press)

P19 Hitler broadcasts to the people, January 1933: (Editors, *Bilder*)

P20 Martin Niemöller: (Verlag Ullstein, Frankfurt/Main)

P21 The manse, 23 Manor Mount, Forest Hill: (Lewisham Local Studies Centre)

P23 Forest Hill, Cobb's Corner (around 1920): (Lewisham Local Studies Centre)

P23 St George's German Church, Sydenham: (Dietrich Bonhoeffer Kirche, Sydenham)

P23 St Paul's Church, Aldgate: (Editors, *Bilder*)

P25 Julius Rieger: (Editors, *Bilder*)

P25 Barnardo's village for children, Barkingside: (Michael Bray)

P26 Trafalgar Square and National Gallery: (Getty Archive)

P29 Baron Bruno Schröder: (By kind permission of George Mallinckrodt KBE, President of Schröders plc)

P30 George Bell, Bishop of Chichester: (WCC Archives, Geneva)

P33 The Athenaeum, Pall Mall, London: (Editors, *Bilder*)

P31 Chichester Cathedral and Palace: (Howard and Jennifer Bottomley)

P33 J.H. Oldham: (WCC Archives, Geneva)

P37 The German Church, Bradford: (Pastor Martin Günther)

P39 Joachim Hossenfelder: (Verlag Ullstein, Frankfurt/Main)

P40 Arthur Cayley Headlam, Bishop of Gloucester with his chaplain Edward Prichard: (Diocese of Gloucester)

P43 Theodor Heckel: (Editors, *Bilder*)

P45 Archbishop Cosmo Gordon Lang: (Hodder & Stoughton)

P46 Lambeth Palace: (Michael Bray)

P46 Lord Lothian, Philip Kerr: (National Portrait Gallery, London)

P48 Bonhoeffer's handwritten translation for Bishop George Bell: (Lambeth Palace Library)

P53 Richard Crossman 1936: (National Portrait Gallery, London)

P55 The Bruay conference, September 1934: (Staatsbibliothek Berlin – Preussischer Kulturbesitz, Nachlass 299 (Bonhoeffer))

P56 J.H Rushbrooke: (Carey Kingsgate Press)

P59 Hans and Gertrud Wedell: (George Wedell)

P61 Eleonora Iredale: (WCC Archives, Geneva)

P62 Dorothy Buxton: (Ben Buxton)

P65 J.H. Oldham's diary: (Oldham Archive, New College, Edinburgh)

P68 *News Chronicle*; the mining disaster at Grassmoor: (British Library Newspapers, Colindale; © *The Daily Mail*, used by permission)

P69 *Daily Telegraph*; the Röhm Putsch: (British Library Newspapers, Colindale; © *The Daily Telegraph*, used by permission)

P71 Perry Rise Baptist Church: (David Hurford)

P72 Bonhoeffer with his confirmands, Ingrid Elisabeth and Gerhard Edward Cruesemann, Palm Sunday 1934: (Dietrich Bonhoeffer Kirche archives, Sydenham)

P730 Auf wiedersehen: the grave of Gertrud Lütgens: (Michael Bray)

P73 The happy couple: Frank Goetz and Doris Dickens: (Rita Colman)

P74 The wedding reception: (Rita Colman)

P76 Mira Behn with Mahatma Gandhi: (Longmans)

P77 Woodbrooke, the Quaker Study Centre at Selly Oak, Birmingham: (Keith Clements)

P79 Richmond College, staff and students 1934-35: (John Rylands Library University of Manchester)

P80 The Africa missionary memorial board, Richmond College: (John Rylands Library University of Manchester)

P82 Playing as well as praying together – a hearty struggle at Spurgeon's College: (Spurgeon's College, London)

P83 Society of St John the Evangelist, Oxford: (Society of St John the Evangelist – "Cowley Fathers")

P83 Bonhoeffer serving: (Staatsbibliothek zu Berlin – Preussischer Kulturbesitz, Nachlass 299 (Bonhoeffer))

P84 Society of the Sacred Mission, Kelham, aerial view: (Society of the Sacred Mission)

P84 Father Herbert Kelly: (Society of the Sacred Mission)

P85 Father Edward Keble Talbot: (Community of the Resurrection, Mirfield)

P86 Walter Howard Frere as Bishop of Truro: (Community of the Resurrection, Mirfield)

P87 Mirfield, Community House of the Resurrection: (Community of the Resurrection, Mirfield)

P87 Mirfield, Church of the Resurrection: (Community of the Resurrection, Mirfield)

Chapter 4 **The Continuing Struggle**

P89 Father Paul Bull: (Community of the Resurrection, Mirfield)

P93 Leonard Hodgson c.1940: (Christopher Hodgson)

P96 Ernst Gordon: (Bettina Gordon)

P97 Sir Walter Moberly: (Sir John Moberly)

P98 Sabine and Gerhard Leibholz at work in their London boarding house: (Editors, *Bilder*)

P99 Dietrich Bonhoeffer with Eberhard Bethge 1939: (Editors, *Bilder*)

P100 Reinhold Niebuhr: (WCC Archives, Geneva)

P100 Bexhill on Sea in the 1930s: (S.B. Publications, Seaford)

P101 Christ Church, Oxford: (Keith Clements)

P103 Platform 1, Paddington Station: (Michael Bray)

P103 W.A. Visser't Hooft: (WCC Archives, Geneva)

P105 Dietrich and Sabine in the garden of their London boarding house: (Editors, *Bilder*)

Chapter 5 **War and Resistance**

P111 Choir of King's College Cambridge, Christmas 1940: (A 'still' from 1940 Ministry of Information film *Christmas Under Fire*. Reproduced by permission of the Archivist, King's College, Cambridge)

P113 William Paton: (WCC Archives, Geneva)

P117 The house on Stora Gatan, Sigtuna: (Keith Clements)

Chapter 6 **From Tegel to Flossenbürg**

P121 Tegel: the view from Bonhoeffer's cell: (Staatsbibliothek zu Berlin – Preussischer Kulturbesitz, Nachlass 299 (Bonhoeffer)).

P121 Bonhoeffer in the courtyard at Tegel Prison

P124 Bonhoeffer's Advent visitors: RAF crews at debriefing after the raid on Berlin 22/23 November 1943: (Imperial War Museum, negative CH 11643. Reproduced by permission)

P125 "Christmas Trees": RAF bombers release their flares over the target area: (Imperial War Museum, negative C.5007. Reproduced by permission)

P127 Buchenwald: (Keith Clements)

P128 Captain Payne Best: (Hutchinson)

P130 Flossenbürg: the execution yard: (Keith Clements)

P130 Schönberg: (Keith Clements)

P131 Flossenbürg: memorial to the resisters executed 9 April 1945: (Keith Clements)

Chapter 7 **Sorrow and Thanksgiving**

P135 Holy Trinity Church, Kingsway: (Michael Bray)

Chapter 8 **A Legacy in Britain**

P139 Ronald Gregor Smith: (The late Dr K. Gregor Smith)

P139 Edwin Robertson: (*Baptist Times*)

P140 Eberhard and Renate Bethge in retirement: (Renate Bethge)

P141 Opening of the Dietrich Bonhoeffer Church, 21 June 1959: (Lewisham Local Studies Centre)

P141 Dietrich Bonhoeffer Church, Sydenham (exterior and interior): (Michael Bray)

P142 Foundation stone of Dietrich Bonhoeffer Church, Sydenham, laid 20 July 1958: (Michael Bray)

P143 M. Leibholz-Bonhoeffer and Jim Dowd, Mayor of Lewisham, at the 'Blue Plaque' unveiling, 9 April 1987

P144 Westminster Abbey: Bonhoeffer stands between Archbishop Oscar Romero of El Salvador and Esther John of Pakistan: (Michael Bray)

Bibliography of Main Sources

1. Works of Dietrich Bonhoeffer

London 1933-1935. Volume 13 of the English edition of the complete Dietrich Bonhoeffer Works, edited by Keith Clements, translated by Isabel Best. Minneapolis: Fortress Press 2006.

Illegale Theologenausbildung: Finkenwalde 1935-1937. Volume 14 of the Bonhoeffer Works. Gütersloh: Chr. Kaiser/Gütersloh Verlagshaus 1996 [in process of translation into English].

Ethics, first English edition, London: SCM Press 1955; new English edition, Volume 6 of the Bonhoeffer Works, Minneapolis: Fortress Press 2004.

No Rusty Swords: Lectures and Notes 1935-39, edited by Edwin Robertson. London: Collins 1965.

The Way to Freedom: Letters, Lectures and Notes 1935-39, edited by Edwin Robertson. London: Collins 1972.

True Patriotism: Letters, Lectures and Notes 1939-45, edited by Edwin Robertson. London: Collins 1973.

Letters and Papers from Prison. London: SCM Press 1971.

2. Works on Dietrich Bonhoeffer

H. Arnold, "Conversations with Dietrich Bonhoeffer", in *The Plough*, no. 8 (1984).

E. Bethge (editor), *Bonhoeffer Gedenkheft.* Berlin: Verlag-Haus und Schule GMBH 1947 [contains the order of the memorial service for Dietrich and Klaus Bonhoeffer, London, 27 July 1945, including the full text of Bishop George Bell's sermon].

E. Bethge, *Dietrich Bonhoeffer. A biography.* Revised edition edited by Victoria Barnett. Minneapolis: Fortress Press 1999.

S. Leibholz-Bonhoeffer, *The Bonhoeffers. Portrait of a family.* London: Sidgwick and Jackson 1971. Re-published Chicago: Covenant Publications 1994.

J. Rieger, *Dietrich Bonhoeffer in England* . Berlin: Lettner-Verlag 1966 [in German].

W-D. Zimmermann and R. Gregor Smith (editors), *I Knew Dietrich Bonhoeffer. Reminiscences by his friends.* London: Collins 1966. [In particular the chapters by F. Hildebrandt, J. Rieger, L.B. Whitburn and W.-D. Zimmermann.]

3. Other works and sources

G. Bell, Christianity *and World Order.* London: Penguin 1940.

P. Best, *The Venlo Incident.* London: Hutchinson 1950.

K. Clements, "A Question of Freedom? British Baptists and the German Church Struggle", in K. Clements (editor), *Baptists in the Twentieth Century*. London: Baptist Historical Society 1983.

K. Clements, *Faith on the Frontier. A life of J.H. Oldham*. London: T. & T. Clark and Geneva: WCC Publications 1999.

J.W. de Gruchy, *Daring, Trusting Spirit. Bonhoeffer's Friend Eberhard Bethge*. Minneapolis: Fortress Press and London: SCM Press 2005.

A. Hastings, *A History of English Christianity 1920-1985*. London: Collins 1986.

Geoffrey Hill, *Collected Poems*. London: Penguin 1985.

L. Hodgson, *Democracy and Dictatorship in the light of Christian Faith*. Oxford: Basil Blackwell 1935.

R.C.D. Jasper, *George Bell: Bishop of Chichester*. London: Oxford University Press 1967.

J.G. Lockhart, *Cosmo Gordon Lang*. London: Hodder & Stoughton 1949.

W. Paton, *The Church and the New Order*. London: SCM Press 1941.

D. Richards, *The Hardest Victory. RAF Bomber Command in the Second World War*. London: Hodder & Stoughton 1994.

R. Roberts, *Schroders. Merchants & Bankers*. London: Macmillan 1992.

R. Rouse and S. Neill (editors), *A History of the Ecumenical Movement 1517-1948*. London: SPCK 1967.

K. Scholder, *The Churches and the Third Reich*. Volume 1, London: SCM Press 1987, Volume 2, London: SCM Press 1988.

W.A. Visser't Hooft, *Memoirs*, 2nd edition, Geneva: WCC Publications 1987.

H. Wedell, *Vom Segen des Glaubens*. Edited by Dietrich Meyer from Archives of the Evangelical Church in the Rhineland: Düsseldorf 1995.

World Alliance for Promoting International Friendship through the Churches: Handbook, reports and press-cuttings on the Cambridge Conference 1931, WCC Archives, Geneva.

WCC Archives, Geneva, on Faith and Order.

Index